With Best W.

Marie Mandell

HEAVEN, MAN AND A CARROT

The Talmud teaches that "the righteous are called living even when they are dead."

DEDICATED

to the memory of
my mother
REBECCA
who was as gentle and devoted as
her biblical namesake

Many men know the laws of mathematics and are skilled in the arts, but most men know very little about the laws governing life, the art of living. One may be able to build an airplane and circle the globe and yet be entirely ignorant of the simple art of how to be happy, successful, and content. When studying the arts, place first upon the list *the art of living*.

Oh, let me converse, Lord, with Thee
From bonds of errors set me free;
And let Thy light within my mind
Remove the shades that keep me blind.

Grant me the power, the right to see,
To love the good and follow Thee;
And in the power, oh, grant the love
Of all on earth, of God above.

HEAVEN, MAN

and a

CARROT

by

MORRIS MANDEL

JONATHAN DAVID • *Publishers*
New York

HEAVEN, MAN and a CARROT
Copyright 1963
by
Morris Mandel

Address all inquiries to Jonathan David, Publishers, 131 East 23 Street, New York 10, N. Y.

Library of Congress Card No. 63-13478

Printed in the United States of America

CONTENTS

TABLE OF CONTENTS—(*continued*)

Preface

A FUSSY traveler was finding much trouble getting settled on the train she and her husband were taking. First, she put her bundles on the seat. Then she changed her mind and moved them to the floor. In a minute or so, she decided she would open the windows. No sooner were they opened than she closed them again. Later, she adjusted the shades. She kept fidgeting about like a nervous hen. When her husband protested, she insisted, "I want to get fixed so I can see the scenery comfortably." He shook his head in obvious dismay and cautioned, "Bessie, we aren't going far and the scenery will be all over before you get fixed to enjoy it."

How true this is of many of us who go through life "getting fixed" to enjoy it—while life passes and is gone. It seems that about the time one learns to make the most of life, most of it is gone. Perhaps it was this that made Bernard Berenson, the great art historian, say, "I wish I could stand on a busy street corner, hat in hand, and beg people to throw me all their wasted hours." The tragedy of life is that many of us tend to put off living. We dream of some beautiful tomorrow, a rose garden over the horizon, instead of enjoying the roses that are blooming in our flower box on the windowsill.

"Life is no brief candle to me," said George Bernard Shaw. "It is a sort of splendid torch which I have got hold of for the moment, and I want to make it burn as brightly as possible before handing it on to future generations." A good rule to follow is to live every day as if it were

the first day we have seen and the last day we are going
to see.

We are in search of happiness and perhaps do not understand that happiness does not come from possessions, but
from our appreciation of them. It does not come from
work but from our attitude toward the work we do. It
does not come from success, but from the spiritual growth
we attain in achieving that success.

Perhaps a lesson in living can be derived from the story
of the artist who decided he wanted to paint the most
beautiful picture in the world. He asked a rabbi, "What
is the most beautiful thing in the world?" "Faith," answered
the rabbi. "Faith makes you stronger. It can be felt in
the synagogue and in the prayers of righteous men."

The artist asked a young bride the same question. "Love,"
she replied. "Love builds poverty into riches; sweetens
tears; makes much of little; makes the grass greener and
the birds sing sweeter. Without love there is no beauty."

A homesick soldier in reply to the same question answered: "Peace is the most beautiful thing in the world.
War is ugly. Wherever you find peace, you find beauty."

The artist now had an answer: *Faith, Love* and *Peace.*
But a new problem arose. "How can I paint them on can-
vas?" he pondered to himself. Entering his home, he saw
faith in the eyes of his children and love in the eyes of
his wife. And there in his home was the peace that love
and faith had built. Now he was able to paint the *most
beautiful thing in the world.* He did, and when he finished
his painting, he called it "Home."

Heaven, Man and a Carrot attempts to point out the
road to happiness. There is no successful life without happiness. Without happiness all living is a failure. This book
should be a heartening one, because it suggests that we
do not have to be defeated in life, that we have it within
our power to achieve happiness and peace of mind. It em-

phasizes that real happiness is a combination of the social, the spiritual, and the personal. Happiness is born the moment we feel we are needed and important. It grows brighter with education and through doing the work we love to do.

All the world is searching for joy and happiness, but these cannot be purchased for any price in any market, because they are virtues that come from within. Like rare jewels, they must be polished, and will shine brightest in the light of faith in God, and when buffed daily in the services of brotherly love.

Heaven, Man and a Carrot advises that we live one day at a time, that we plan for tomorrow and hope for the future, but that we don't live in it. It counsels that to find happiness we must be willing to ignore what life owes us and think about what we owe life.

Many people have been helpful in the preparation of this work, and I take this opportunity to express my sense of indebtedness to them: Sam Klaus for his practical everyday living, Rabbi Menachem Kasher for his spiritual and scholarly inspiration, Rabbi Mel Heftler for his rabbinic parables, Dr. Eli Gottesman for his contagious enthusiasm, Leo Gartenberg for his moral illustrations, and Jacob Schechter for his words of wisdom. I am grateful to the publishers and their staff for their interest and counsel, and to my dear wife Shirley, for careful editing through all the stages of publication, and for her painstaking constructive criticism which was of enormous help to me in the preparation of this book. Last but not least, I wish to express a word of tribute to my son Allen for reading the manuscript and suggesting that its title be *Heaven, Man and a Carrot*.

MORRIS MANDEL

Brooklyn, New York
February 1963

CHAPTER ONE

Heaven, Man and a Carrot

HAVE you ever seen the old-fashioned scales that were used years ago to weigh grocery products? They were quite different from the scales used today. On each end of these old-fashioned scales a scoop swung free. Weights were placed on one side of the scales, while goods which were to be sold were placed on the other side. When the scales balanced perfectly, the merchant knew the weight of the merchandise.

A rabbi once dreamed about such a set of scales, and in his dream, the scales were tremendous. In fact, they were suspended from Heaven so all the men and women of the world could see them. Thousands of angels heaped valuables upon valuables on the left side of these scales. Angels were busy gathering all the gold stored in national treasuries and collecting all the precious gems from the productive mines of the world. Coal, oil, gold, lumber, ivory, diamonds, spices—everything of value was added to the mountainous heap of increasing wealth. As this was done, the side of the scales with the piles of valuables dipped and dipped until it almost touched the earth, and the other side of the scales slowly disappeared into the heavens. The rabbi noticed the people stare in amazement as they asked one another, "How could these scales ever be made to balance?"

Then a strange thing happened. It was unusual and totally unexpected. From somewhere in Heaven, hands appeared, gently holding a "heart." This heart was placed on the right side of the scales. As the people stared, the left

1

side began to waver, and slowly but surely rose in the air until it was so tipped that all the precious things—the gold and diamonds—were in danger of spilling out on the ground. Then the rabbi heard a Heavenly voice proclaim, "The heart of an individual is more precious than all the valuables in the world."

Rightly so! Without a heart a person is only an animal with clothes. The heart differentiates between people and animals. It is the inner chamber of a human being through which a person grows and functions.

Man, because of his great capacity for learning, is the most adaptable creature in the world. He has learned to adjust to his environment; to live in the cold arctic and in the sweltering heat of equatorial lands. He has learned to fly through the air like a bird; to swim across the oceans like a fish. He has conquered the earth, the air, the seas. Now he is faced with a far greater challenge, upon which the fate of the world rests. He must learn to conquer himself. Perhaps when he successfully meets this challenge, he will learn to walk upon this earth like a human being.

Paul Dore, the great French artist, was wandering through the Swiss Alps and was stopped by a government official who demanded to see his passport papers. Dore tried to explain who he was and said that he had left his passport at the hotel. The official was skeptical, but finally said, "If you are Paul Dore you can readily demonstrate it by painting a picture of this landscape." Whereupon Dore unpacked his equipment and proceeded to paint a beautiful scene. On observing the great skill with which Dore painted, the official said, "Indeed, it is plain to see that you are Paul Dore."

The poet with his musical rhyme and meter says:
"Praise not thy work, but let thy work praise thee,
   For deeds, not words, make each man's memory stable;

If what thou dost is good, it good all men will see;
Musk by its smell is known, not by its label."
There was once a beautiful clock which had kept ticking
away for many years. It had ticked for grandma and
grandpa, for mother and father. It ticked accurately and
dependably. But there was one thing wrong with this beautiful clock; it had no hands. One could hear the regular
tick-tock, tick-tock, but the face of the clock said nothing,
because the hands were gone. The insides of the clock were
in perfect running order, but the outside was of no help
to anyone.

There are people who can be compared to this clock.
They claim they are good on the inside. "My heart's in
the right place," they quickly tell you, but their actions do
not prove their words. Lip service is valueless because life
is based on action rather than on intent, and judgment is
made on deeds, not words.

The purpose of life is not just to live, but to be productive, to be useful, to be of help to humanity, to leave an
imprint on the universe. It is ever true that the life one
lives speaks more loudly than the words one utters.

The character of a person is judged by his capacity to
see others as human beings and treat them so. The world
today is seeking men who are sincere, honest, and sound
from center to circumference, and true to the heart's core.
One of God's greatest gifts to man has been to endow him
with the ability to communicate his knowledge, his emotions, and his understanding. Character grows in the soil
of human relations, fertilized by example, nurtured by
giving, and warmed by love for mankind.

There is a story told about a man who died and went
where he belonged. He found the place not at all to his
liking. His quarters were hot, hotter than he had anticipated. His bed was most uncomfortable. He griped and

complained continuously. In great desperation, he finally cried out, "Please get me out of this place!"

An angel heard his cry and asked him what he had ever done to merit a better resting place. After much pondering and soul-searching the man replied, "I remember once giving a carrot to a half-starved donkey."

"Good," replied the angel, "I believe I now have the means to help you." No sooner were these words out of the angel's mouth than an immense carrot was lowered from Heaven and a Voice cried out, "Take hold of the carrot and you will be saved."

The man needed no second invitation. He seized the carrot which began to carry him up to Heaven. Hundreds of souls saw this miracle. They, too, wanted to be saved, so they hurried to take hold of the carrot, and began to rise with him. Then the man's true nature asserted itself and he shouted, "Let go there! This is my carrot. Go get your own carrot if you want to be saved!" Immediately, the carrot dropped and the man returned to his original destination.

Selfishness mirrors weakness of character and sooner or later develops an undesirable personality. People who live a self-centered life generally are left to themselves, for they hang a "NO TRESPASSING" sign on their hearts. In truth, selfishness is a dead-end street. The man who lives for himself alone is a failure; the man who lives for others as well, achieves true success.

Years ago, Alfred Adler advised, "It is the individual who is not interested in his fellow men who has the greatest difficulties in life. It is from among such individuals that all human failures spring." Could it not be added that what poison is to food, selfishness is to life?

Life is monotonous and dull to us until we begin to discover the vast treasures within us, which may be used to help others. It is normal for man to try to earn a sufficient income for himself and to build an adequate home for his family. However, he can gain great satisfaction from helping others while busying himself with his personal needs. Opportunities for helping others present themselves each day. A sick woman needs company and soft comforting words. A depressed middle-aged man needs cheering because business has been going downhill and he feels that he is a failure. A hospital can use the help of volunteers in many capacities—feeding the handicapped, reading to the ill.

A youngster with a mirror was seen throwing rays of sunshine toward the upper story of a house. An old man nearby was curious and asked why he was doing it. "I'm throwing a little sunshine up in Yankel's room. He's my pal. He broke his leg last week and today is our school debate and Yankel can't be with us—so I'm sending him a little sunshine to let Yankel know that we're thinking of him."

The real wealth of a person does not lie in his bank balances and resources, nor in the securities placed in his safe-deposit vault. These have only been loaned to him and some day will have to be returned to the donor. The true wealth of a person lies in his hidden strength—his desire to help others without recompense. The best exercise for strengthening the heart is to reach down and lift others up. Happiness is sought for in various ways, but it is always present when one has done something for another.

We make a living by what we get; we make a life by what we give.

CHAPTER TWO

How to Be a Human Being

"WHERE art thou?" That is the question the Lord put to Adam who had hidden himself after eating the fruit of the forbidden tree. Our Sages ask: "If the Lord knew everything and could see everywhere, why did He ask Adam where he was?" The answer given is, "When the Lord asked Adam, 'Where art thou,' He didn't mean, where art thou physically. He meant: And now where do you stand, Adam? How have you committed yourself?"

You may not be an Emerson, Leonardo da Vinci, Maimonides, Rashi. They surpass the average person in the quality of creativity. Their creations are appreciated by millions. But even if you are not so highly gifted, your creations may be appreciated and bring new insights concerning life, to yourself and your family.

One may ask, "What is creativity?" It is a process based on curiosity, inventiveness, the urge for discovery and exploration. It is an expression of spontaneous uniqueness, freedom, individuality, and originality. The truth is that great men have but a few hours to be "great." Like the rest of us, they must dress, pray, eat and sleep. And being human, they too must visit the dentist, the doctor and the barber. They too must spend time with their wives and children. The thing that makes them great is their willingness to focus their attention on important matters which they have learned to love.

To do great work, you must fall in love with what you are doing. Cellini, the goldsmith, poured his whole soul into

his creations and achieved masterpieces which brought him
the praise of kings. Work that is done in the spirit of love
glows with a quality no one can explain. Robert Louis
Stevenson summarized it best when he said, "I know what
happiness is, for I have done good work."

Love of work generates ideas, and ideas generate new
ideas. The more ideas you have and share, the more you
receive. A trained mind continually creates. The ability to
generate new ideas is something that no one can take from
you. And after all, an idea is the only lever which really
moves the world.

The story is told that Paganini owned a wonderful
Stradivarius, a violin that made people laugh or cry, made
them feel the warmth of the sun, or hear the patter of
the rain. He willed this remarkable instrument to an Italian
city, with the provision that it should never be played.
The violin was displayed for all to see in an exquisite
case studded with diamonds. Today, all that remains of
that violin is the case. The violin itself is a small heap of
dust. Wood, if used even so slightly, remains strong. Neglected, it turns to dust.

God has given you certain times to do certain things:
to learn particular facts, to achieve individual skills, to
develop unique traits of character. You must do the right
thing at the right time because, unlike a practice baseball
game, you can't repeat life.

The first assignment given to you at birth is the *struggle
for survival*. You must learn to walk, talk, feed, clean, and
defend yourself. This subsequently involves earning a living,
sharing your life with others, and becoming part of a
throbbing community.

As you go through life you learn lessons through trial,
error, and crisis. You receive warnings that frighten, pun-
ishments that antagonize, admonishments that create guilt

feelings, threats that make you cautious, unfulfilled promises that make you suspicious, and failures that anger. Yet, somehow, you survive, and indicate to the world that you have developed the "know-how" for survival. That is to say, you receive passing grades at school; make a living; find a suitable mate; establish a home; rear children responsibly; contribute to society. But this is not enough to make you enjoy the full excitement that can be the reward of adult living. For this you must add to the struggle for survival the *struggle towards goals*. In other words, you must commit yourself to the truths in which you believe. To do this you must come to terms with your past, because only then can you be in a position to take a stand about your present and a chance on your future. It is at this moment that you are asked: *"Where art thou?"* It is then that life flings to you the challenge to commit yourself, so that you may fulfill your deepest needs.

There is the familiar story of the man who found it hard to locate his clothing upon arising in the morning. One evening he took paper and pencil and, as he undressed, noted down where he placed his clothes. The next morning he took the slip of paper in hand and read: "Cap is on the chair. Pants and jacket are in the closet. Shoes are under the bed." He dressed and looked at the last item on the list, which read: "I am in bed." He began to search for himself and after a while cried out in frustration, "I have found everything that belongs to me, but what good is it when I myself am lost!"

A person's fate, to a great extent, will be what he decides it can be. He need not be lost. The trouble with many of us is that we don't have to turn out the lights to be in the dark. We stumble daily because we are groping in the dark, because we do not know where we are going. Every human being has the potentiality for creativity.

In reality, where are we, what is the use of living, if not to work for noble causes and to make this muddled world a better place in which our children may dwell after we are gone? And what tools do we have to work with other than our own natural resources? To succeed we must use what we have.

Thank God for your talents and abilities. Accept them as a treasure to be invested for the common good of society. Remember that time is the essence of life. Tomorrow is now. Don't procrastinate any longer by putting off today what you should have done yesterday, last week, last month, last year.

A young lawyer was asked by his former teacher at the university what he had accomplished in his city during his first five years of practice. The young man replied that he still hadn't got around to do much for justice there. The teacher was displeased with the answer, and asked, "When you light a candle do you expect it to give light after it is half burned, or when you first light it?" "As soon as I light it," was the quick reply, and with his answer the young man understood the point that was being made.

In this world of tension, in this age of anxiety, when someone else's decision may lead to the destruction of the world in which you live, you are asked to come out of hiding and take a stand. You are called upon to indicate to others the kind of person you really are and to identify the purpose of your life. Your responsibility is to commit yourself.

There must be preparation to take up the challenge that life eventually demands. Take inventory of strengths, not weaknesses. Think of successes, not failures. Think of the times you rose above the usual and perfected an idea or a dream you had deeply longed to fulfill. Think of the big moments in your life. These are the pictures you should have in mind as you go through life.

There was once a man who believed that India rubber could be made useful. People laughed at him, but for eleven years he struggled with hardship to make his dream come true. His neighbors called him insane, but Charles Goodyear persevered. His success is well known.

A true individual faces life with courage, and realizes that life is a struggle for future goals. It is not enough to have a good aim in life; you must also pull the trigger. Accept all your experiences, impulses, feelings, failures and successes with the recognition that it really rests within yourself to choose your own way of life. Make it your real concern to find an honest answer to the question: "Is this way of living satisfying to me and does it really express me as a person?"

In the final analysis, remember, man cannot live by his own strength alone.

CHAPTER THREE

Facing a Challenge

WHEN confronted with a problem that you fear may be difficult to answer, do you reach for a tranquilizer, a pillow, a cocktail? If you do, you are less afraid of the problem than you are to face the disagreeable, painful sensations of a new challenge. Being unwilling to cope with the problems that confront you, you seek to deaden the dread feeling of anxiety.

Anxiety is to the mind what the appendix is to the body. Seldom doing much good and capable of causing great harm, anxiety can be a deadly enemy which is responsible for many physical and mental ailments, for it precipitates failure due to the anticipation of failure.

Anxiety is not always neurotic. Many people work within an anxiety strait-jacket. Some wear it very tightly and some wear it loosely. How each person meets new challenges determines whether the anxiety he feels is considered "normal" or "neurotic."

Dr. Girrard Franklin, associate psychologist at the Postgraduate Center for Psychotherapy, states, "Anxiety is a condition of uncertainty which gives rise to painful feelings of possible helplessness that occur whenever a person is faced with an unfamiliar threat to his essential security." A threat of this nature is a fundamental challenge to an individual's self-respect because it questions the extent of his effectiveness as a human being.

Sam is a qualified bookkeeper. He earned excellent grades in his high school and business school accounting courses

11

and is capable of performing the duties of a bookkeeper. He is neat and accurate. Yet, when applying for a job, he is convinced beforehand that he will never be hired, or will not be able to keep the position for any length of time. This uncertainty and doubt cannot be considered normal behavior.

Mary is an attractive young lady. She is intelligent, loves to read, and is interested in many activities. Her college instructors feel she is in the upper half of the class. Yet, she is plagued with the thought, "How can anyone really like me?" This might be termed neurotic anxiety.

Harry does hours and hours of homework. Before each examination he spends days of intensive studying. He keeps careful notebooks of all lectures attended. His term papers always indicate careful preparation. Yet, he is overcome with the conviction that all his efforts will end in failure. He is filled with vague feelings of helplessness. Since the outcome seems so discouraging before he even begins his examination, it is evident that he will be unable to do his best.

To whom can you compare yourself—Sam, Mary, or Harry? The tragedy is that if you can compare yourself to any of the three, you are imposing on yourself limitations which actually bring about failure. You are restricting your talents and capacities. It is similar to driving a car in low gear with the brakes on. Very little if any progress can be made.

And so, you, Sam, Mary, or Harry resort to tranquilizers, or to drinks, or to the extra cigarette. Or perhaps you attempt to sleep your troubles away. Temporarily, you experience some relief but it is at the expense of genuine satisfaction in accepting a challenge.

Though a man garbs himself in expensive clothing, accumulates wealth and gains power over people, his self-image breaks through and determines to a great extent what he will do with and make of himself. What a man feels he is, shapes his behavior. "All things in the world follow thought," teaches the Holy Bible. "Every deed of a man is in his heart." Scripture then describes the heart as seeing, understanding, and hearing.

"Wishing Won't Make It So," the title of a popular song some years ago, suggested that the struggle to hold persistently in mind what we yearn and pray for, makes us what we are. Just as we can plunge into inferiority through apathy and pessimism, we can soar to the heights through enthusiasm and optimism. We cannot hope to catch lions if we think in terms of catching mice.

Why do some people fail as others succeed?

Self-trust and self-confidence are the secrets of success. Every human being has something to contribute to society, and he should not permit cares and anxieties to dull the enthusiasm of creating. He should take an objective look at his values, and not underrate his abilities. If there is a great deal of good in him, he will discover it.

A rabbi tells the story of two bakers in a small town. One of them came to the rabbi to inform him that he was going to close his bakery and move elsewhere.

"Why are you closing up shop?" inquired the rabbi, hoping perhaps to be of some service to his troubled congregant.

"You see, rabbi," replied the depressed store-keeper, "my competitor gets a good deal of the business; most of the customers seem to go into his bakery."

"How do you know that most of the townsmen go to his store?" inquired the rabbi.

"It's quite simple. When I stand at my door, I see many people entering and leaving his bake-shop."

"That's just the trouble," answered the wise rabbi. "If you were not so intent on watching his store, but spent time building your reputation, success might be yours."

Failure in life may be due to deficiencies in the person himself—a weak constitution, poor environment, improper training or unhealthy attitudes. It may be expressed in business reverses, disappointment and dissatisfaction in one's career, or family quarrels and disintegration, and leads to an inability to face new challenges, to a decline in religious faith. Life holds little meaning for hearts burdened by unnecessary worry and sorrow.

Life is largely a matter of determination and courage. A troubled heart cannot see the glories of tomorrow. A wise man once said, "I am only one; but I am one. I cannot do everything but I can do something. What I can do, I ought to do; and what I ought to do, by the grace of God I will do."

A positive philosophy of life will help people keep their integrity and face heroically whatever life holds in store for them. "Cast out fear," says Emerson. "Rely on your own inner resources; trust life and it will repay your trust. You can do better than you believe you can." The basic objective of living is to become a mature person. Because the process of growing up wisely challenges man's resourcefulness, much time and patience are necessary to build the ideal personality. A person should aim at constant improvement—not perfection. A person must face reality with enthusiasm and understand that he cannot control all of life.

On the walls of an ancient temple this picture was found: A king was forging a chain from his crown, while nearby a slave was making a crown out of his chains. Underneath was written: "Life is what man makes of it, no matter of what it is made."

A successful code for living, simply stated, is this:

Face up to new challenges!

Know your real worth! While you shouldn't over-estimate yourself, it is advantageous to realize your potentialities. Success is never a gift or accident, but rather the result of careful planning in a positive frame of mind, accompanied by enthusiastic and accurate execution.

Hard work is the best investment a man can make, and the love of work will stimulate creativity, until genuine happiness is experienced in one's accomplishments. Any activity can be either sheer drudgery or a pleasurable occupation, depending on how you regard it.

Karl Menninger, a noted psychiatrist, once summed up the difference between work and play this way: "The psychiatrist plays at being a photographer, the professional photographer plays at being a horticulturist, the florist plays at being a carpenter, the carpenter plays at being an artist, the artist plays at being a cook, and the cook may, along with several million blithe spirits, be playing at being a psychiatrist." The individual's attitude toward an activity can transform it from grim drudgery to gay fun, or vice-versa.

It has been said, "A man without judgment is like a car without brakes; but a man without enthusiasm is like a car without a motor." The man who has done his best has done everything. The man who has done less than his best has done nothing.

"The heights by great men reached and kept,
Were not attained by sudden flight,
But they, while their companions slept,
Were toiling upward in the night."

CHAPTER FOUR

Pattern for Living

A ARON arrived home after a difficult day at the office.
Things had not gone right. Stock prices fell during
a slump in the market. Large orders, expected for days,
had not materialized. Tedious conferences had not produced
satisfactory solutions to perplexing business questions. Eating dinner had been a real effort. Troubled and bewildered,
Aaron fell asleep and dreamed.

In his dream he saw two bundles—one marked *"happiness"* and a larger one marked, *"unhappiness."* For a moment Aaron gazed at one and then at the other. Suddenly,
in alarm, he lashed out at the bundle marked *"unhappiness,"*
clawing at it again and again, struggling desperately to
puncture it and release its burden. But to no avail. It remained solid and resistant. Frustrated, he lifted imploring
eyes heavenward. At this moment he seemed to hear a
voice proclaim, "You must take an intelligent and determined stand if you wish to save the world from impending
doom. Create happiness in your life and in the lives of
those close to you and the bundle of *"unhappiness"* may
disappear."

A large balance of happiness is the dream of most
people. Some of us seek it in the form of money. Others
who have money seek it in the form of power.

Life is short . . . too short for most of us. There is
so much to do, so much to see, so much to learn, and so
little time in which to accomplish our aims. Yet, we observe
men and women who are too lazy to fulfill life's tasks.

They wildly chase after material pleasures as if death would remove them tomorrow, and they postpone the pursuit of real goals as if an eternity were at their disposal. They insist that today's wealth and tomorrow's promises are the things that really matter. They are not aware that by following this rule they make their lives poorer, because so much of what is done today is frivolous, futile, and soon forgotten; and so much of that which is planned for tomorrow just never happens. They live in a world where most of their wants represent physical luxury and nothing more. It was this type of living that Elijah Gaon referred to when he said: "This mundane life is like a drink of salt water, which seems to quench, but actually in flames."

If men and women conducted businesses the way they run their lives, their creditors would be knocking at the doors of the bankruptcy court. Fortunately, when a man organizes a business he seeks the advice of experts—accountants, lawyers, investment counselors. He leaves no stone unturned to make certain that he is investing wisely, since he realizes that prosperity is the result of thorough preparation and planning.

The business of life must be planned as well. Someone asked his friend: "If you were shipwrecked, alone, on a distant island, and could have one book, which one would you choose?" The friend wisely replied, "Johnson's Manual of Ship Building!"

A philosophy, embodying a plan for living, gives a person the perspective to realize life's goals and to see trivialities and superficialities for what they are. A blueprint for living prevents a person from being upset over small matters when greater, more important issues are at stake. Everyone who eats, walks, breathes, who complains about his work, family and friends is alive. It does not follow, however, that he knows the art of living.

There is a gift that each of us is given at birth. The gift is withheld from no man. Some of us leave the package unclaimed; others take the package and carry it around, but fail to remove the wrappings and discover the inner treasure. The packages we inherit are all alike: in each case the owner finds an allotment of years, marked with this inscription, *take these and live.*

Unfortunately, we are too busy complaining about our legacy. We feel we have not inherited as rich an inheritance as we would have liked to receive. The question for each of us to settle is not what we would do if we had means, time, influence, beauty and educational advantages, but what we could do with the things we have. Those who accept their legacy, actually get more out of life than those who complain. It is a law of life that we generally become what we fix our attention upon. Life is what we make it. Nothing in life is surer than this. What a man believes in, what he is willing to struggle for, helps shape the future he will have. Life is a jug given to us to fill; a busy life fills it with as much as it can hold, a hurried life has had more poured into it than it can contain.

The great scholar Hillel pointed out the faults of an over-emphasized material existence when he said that the mad pursuit for material wealth and its acquisition resulted in grave disappointment. This he illustrated with the much quoted statement in *Perek,* ". . . the more property, the more anxiety . . . , the more Torah, the more life; the more schooling, the more wisdom; the more counsel, the more understanding. . . ." Hillel stressed that spiritual pursuits, when finally realized, bring lasting happiness. Lofty values should be the motivation in life.

How can we make each day a complete one? How can we live on this earth so that we can derive the greatest possible satisfaction? How can we really leave "footprints on the sands of time?"

The wealthy man says, "Amass a fortune."

The poet advises, "Write an epic poem."

The actor claims, "Be a star in a hit show and see your name in lights."

The school-child says, "Pass all tests with high marks."

Many rules for the good life have been given both in religious and in secular writings. Long ago, Socrates wrote above a Greek temple, "Know thyself," for he realized that the art of living depended upon an accurate knowledge of oneself. The modern teacher has altered this to read "Behave thyself." The psychologist changes this to "Be thyself."

The religious leader says, "Be content with thy lot," for he knows that with contentment comes happiness and with happiness comes a true appreciation of life. Over and over again people have summarized the goal of life as the "pursuit of happiness." *Live today, tomorrow may never come* is the motto of men and women alike. Granted, happiness is an important ingredient in life. However, a person who uses his intelligence constructively stands a better chance of achieving happiness, for he understands that *thrills* are not the same as *enduring satisfactions;* that *happiness* and *pleasure* are not synonyms, and that one's own happiness is tied up with the happiness of other people.

The understanding person identifies himself with civic groups, religious groups, social groups and service organizations. He is strengthened in the conviction that his life counts for something. This is a prescription that psychiatrists and psychologists often advise a patient to follow. "Man's value is to grow," they teach. "When he is not able to grow, the dynamic life process that works within him doubles back upon itself and casts its energies into disorder. The result is confusion accompanied by the symptoms of disoriented living that have been diagnosed in modern times as neurosis. The choice before man is thus one of extremes: either growth with its fullness of rewards in life, or stalemate with growing restlessness, confusion, and eventual breakdown."

Unfortunately, some merely set out to purchase happiness. But he who believes that the possession of expensive cars, clothing, jewels will bring happiness ultimately learns that there is little satisfaction in being the owner of material assets only. The Vilna Gaon, years ago, pointed out, "What gives you pleasure today will make you weak tomorrow. Neither be zealous after glory which is likewise a vain thing."

With this in mind, the individual must choose as his life's occupation something that will give him satisfaction in ways other than those of a monetary nature. He should feel that there is a purpose underlying his work. A sense of competence in his profession would add greatly to the joy of working. "Every craftsman and artist," said Eleazar b. Azariah, "takes pride in his work." On the wall of his office, Dr. Charles Mayo kept the following motto: "There is no fun like work."

"I have always liked this motto," he once remarked, "for I believe it. To be without work is almost to be without life, for it is work which creates interest in life." In *Genesis Rabbah* we read, "Weeds spring up of themselves and thrive; but to produce wheat, how much toil and trouble must be endured." A man's life may be compared to the growth of weeds or wheat. The "weed" produces nothing of value. He has no useful purpose in life—is just an aimless drifter. No doubt his loved ones will mourn him, but society will not miss him. He spent his life satisfying selfish desires, denying spiritual or intellectual development. The "wheat" shows genuine worth, is productive, and will live on in the lives of others.

A person with an active philosophy searches for values in which he can believe and work. He believes that the universe is good and that justice will ultimately prevail; that life can be rich if it is inspired by love and guided by wisdom; that there is in Heaven a loving Father; that prayer is effective; and that there is immortality.

In *Proverbs*, we read

> "Happy is the man that hearkeneth to me
> Watching daily at my gates,
> Waiting at the posts of my doors."

How can one be happy? Let him be contented with his lot. Let him love those close to him. Let him forgive and forget past hurts. Let him cast away envy from his gates. Let him overlook his neighbor's faults. Let him forget slander. Let him forget petty personal quarrels. Let him erase everything disagreeable from yesterday and not nurture hatred.

Happiness begins in the home. Since environment helps shape personality, a child brought up in surroundings of joy will have a better chance of becoming a happy adult. A child reared in an environment of security will have a greater opportunity of growing into a secure individual. The Vilna Gaon, in his ethical will, stated, "The aim of the Torah in large part was to induce a desire for happiness." The advice given was, "Let there be no dissention of any kind among all the household, men and women, but let love and brotherliness reign."

Wisdom is happiness. In *Proverbs*, Solomon states, "Happy is the man that findeth wisdom, and the man that obtaineth understanding. For the merchandise of it is better than the merchandise of silver and the gain thereof better than fine gold."

There is an art in enjoying the blessings of life—a realization that everything we are, and everything we have, are gifts from the Creator. With this in mind, joy in possession deepens and deprivation lightens.

Finally, it would seem that the secret of happiness is for man to learn to like what he has to do—to adjust himself to his environment rather than the environment to him.

A worried college instructor was speaking to the president of the university about the large number of unappreciative and unhappy people in the world today. "Maybe," the president suggested, "these people have been given too much to live with and not enough to live for."

CHAPTER FIVE

Time: Your Most Precious Asset

FROM the hands of God, you receive the gift of life—
an allotted time to be spent on this earth. How many
years this will be no one can know for certain. Nor does
God indicate to His children the nature of His reward for
their efforts on earth.

Our sages relate a parable: There was a wealthy man
who hired laborers and brought them into his orchard. He
assigned to them the work of pruning and nursing a variety
of trees. Each worker was permitted to select the type of
tree which appealed to him. They worked diligently. When
evening came the rich man called them all together and
asked each one, "At which tree have you worked?" One
pointed out a pepper tree; he was given a gold coin. One
who had worked on a white-blossom tree was given half a
gold piece. Another who had worked on an olive tree was
given 200 zuz.

The laborers who had received the smaller sums were
disgruntled. "If you had told us in the beginning," they
argued, "for which tree there would be the higher pay,
each of us might have had the opportunity to work on it."

The rich man replied, "Each of you selected the type of
work you wanted to do. Had I told you about the rewards
offered, perhaps my entire orchard would not have been
pruned and nursed."

The parable is instructive. It is a guide to living. God
does not indicate the reward that He will grant to man for
labor performed. Each person must select the type of work

he prefers and work at it hard and long. *Time*, the years
of one's life, must be spent profitably. It must not be
wasted. The person who loves life does not squander time,
for that is the stuff life is made of.

Arnold Bennett wrote: "The supply of time is a daily
miracle. . . . You wake up in the morning, and lo! your
purse is magically filled with twenty-four hours of the manufactured tissue of the universe of life. It is yours! the
most precious of your possessions. No one can take it from
you and no one receives more or less than you receive."
Time is the essence of life. The wealth of time is like gold
in the mine, like the gem in the pebble, like the pearl in
the deep. The mine must be worked, the pebble ground and
polished, the deep fathomed and searched.

You cannot wait until tomorrow, for tomorrow is now.
The poet tells us,

> "I have no yesterdays, time took them away;
> Tomorrow may not be—but I have today."

Sanhedrin (110b) cautions,

> "About the morrow do not sorrow!
> For thee there may be no tomorrow.
> Thou mayest find thou didst but pine
> About a world that was not thine."

Time lost is gone forever. Omar Khayam points out the
value of time in the *Rubaiyat*:—

> "The moving Finger writes, and having writ,
> moves on: nor all your Piety nor Wit
> Shall lure it back to cancel half a Line,
> Nor all your Tears wash out a Word of it."

Too many people fritter away their lives with a thousand
details of which nine hundred get them nowhere—certainly

not any nearer to happiness. Horace Mann bemoaned the serious loss in lives when he wrote, "Lost yesterday, somewhere between sunrise and sunset, two golden hours, each set with sixty diamond minutes. No reward is offered for they are gone forever."

A confirmation of this thought is found in *Berachot* (3) : "The passing of a day into night occurs in the twinkling of an eye." Time cannot be expanded, accumulated, mortgaged, hastened or retarded. It is the one thing completely beyond man's control. Said an eighty-year-old man, "I wish I could stand on a busy street corner and beg people to give me all their wasted hours."

Time is more precious than gold. Each new hour is a new opportunity for aspiration, for endeavor, and for achievement; for adding something to the world's wealth, and to one's own growth. Time, even in its smallest units of hours and minutes, is the raw material of all human achievement. Every hour of every day offers you a just reward for what is done. Every grain of sand as it drops to the lower half of the hourglass is a part of your life. Once it is gone, it can never be recalled. When you waste time you waste life—your own.

Take time to live, it's one secret of success.
Take time to think, it's the source of power.
Take time to play, it's the secret of youth.
Take time to read, it's the foundation of knowledge.
Take time for friendship, it's the source of happiness.
Take time to laugh, it helps lift life's lot.
Take time to dream, it hitches the soul to the stars.

A good bit of advice in the same direction comes from Philip J. Bailey. He writes, "We live in deeds, not years; in thoughts, not breaths; in feelings, not in figures on a dial. We should count time by heart throbs. He most lives who thinks most, feels the noblest, acts the best."

It is possible for you to give the gift of time—the time it takes to do your job conscientiously; the time it takes to offer a sincere compliment; the time it takes to think twice before you say an unkind word, and then not say it at all. Unfortunately, a person realizes the full importance of time only when there is little of it left. There was an ancient custom of putting an hour-glass into the coffin of the dead to signify that their time had run out, a useless notification to them. It would have been more beneficial to put the hour-glass into the hand of every living man, and show them the grains trickling steadily out, the passing of a lifetime. Lost wealth may be restored by industry, the wreck of health regained by diet and rest, forgotten knowledge restored by study, evil conquered by penitence and virtue; but no one can ever look again upon his vanished hours, recall his wasted years, efface from Heaven's record the blot of wasted time.

"How do you spend your time?" We all speak about spending time. But did you ever stop to think of what that means? You are given a certain amount of time—24 hours a day. All this time must be used. You must *spend* it—buy things with it. You cannot save any of it for another day.

What can you purchase with this capital which you receive each day? What can you purchase when you spend your allotment of time? You can buy many things—information, skill, friendship, culture, recreation. You can broaden your interests, develop your personality, prepare for success. Or you may squander your time just as you may squander money which is given you. You may spend time wisely or foolishly. But spend it you must.

What do you spend your time for each day? You may spend about a third of it sleeping. You can't very well avoid that. You may spend about a twelfth of it eating. You spend hours going to and from work. With some of your time, you buy the pleasures which come from conversation, or from the movies, or hobbies.

But do these things take up all your time? How much do you spend merely for the privilege of loafing? How much do you actually waste for things which leave you bored rather than stimulated?

In these days of large scale production and efficient management, the success of a business often depends upon utilizing the so-called "by-products" of the main item manufactured. For example, there are many by-products in the meat industry—brushes, ropes, buttons, fertilizers. There is no doubt that meat packers would show a decrease in profit if they did not make use of their by-products.

You may not be a business man but you are a dealer in time. This is an asset which you wholly possess, and your success depends upon the use of your time. It is true that you have a regular day's work that you are called upon to do. You may be a painter, grocer, carpenter, typist, and must put in a certain number of hours daily at your chosen vocation. But does that end your day?

What about the by-product, the spare moment? The successful men in this world are those who have wisely used spare moments. Edison, for example, was hammering away at a telegraph-key when he was a salaried telegraph-operator. However, he didn't neglect the by-product. He thought and planned between messages. It was in his spare moments, early in life, that he thought of the many inventions that gave him millions and the world a life of luxury. He used his extra time productively.

Every minute saved by using it profitably is so much added to your life and its possibilities. Every minute lost is a neglected by-product; once gone it can never be regained. A declaration of insolvency was made by the man who confessed, "All my life I have been planning, hoping, thinking, dreaming and waiting. All my life I have been getting ready to do something worthwhile. I have been waiting for the summer, and waiting for the fall; I've been waiting for the spring—waiting, dawdling and dreaming— until the year is almost spent." Rabbi Tarphon said, "The day is short, the work is great, the laborers are sluggish, the reward is much, and the Master of the house urges one on." It is only too true that as you advance in life, you acquire a keener sense of the value of time, desiring to hoard it like a miser.

The poetic words of Thomas Carlyle almost plead:

> "So here hath been dawning
>   Another blue day;
> Think, wilt thou let it
>   Slip useless away?

> "Out of Eternity
>   This new day is born;
> Into Eternity
>   At night, will return.

> "Before it aforetime
>   No eye ever did;
> So soon it forever
>   From all eyes is hid.

> "Here hath been dawning
>   Another blue day;
> Think, wilt thou let it
>   Slip useless away?"

CHAPTER SIX

Accept the Challenge

IF fate were to confront us suddenly with the chance of a lifetime, could we accept the challenge? Could we summon all our powers and courage and go forth and greet the new experience? Tragically, for too many of us, the answer is "No!" Instead, we use every resource at our command to avoid our true destiny. We even delude ourselves into believing that we never had the chance.

Why should this happen? Perhaps we are faced with the problem of encountering fate alone and are lacking in self-confidence. We find ourselves clinging to the "status quo," frustrated and disappointed.

In the words of Dr. Edgar M. Foss of the Postgraduate Center for Psychotherapy, "So many of us find ourselves bobbing up and down on the ripples of the river of life, together with the chance aggregation of whatever flotsam and jetsam is present, nudged along by every current and breeze, making no effort to paddle in a direction of our own choosing." As a result we find ourselves without the very things we crave and need the most for fulfillment: a love relationship, achievement commensurate with our innate abilities in a field we respect, and the birth of our real selves.

Satan once decided to rid himself of some of the tools he had been using for years. He felt he could now do his job just as well without them, so he arranged to run an auction sale. The tools he offered for sale were envy, prejudice, malice, deceit, hatred. These carried low price tags.

In contrast, one piece, labeled *discouragement* was marked very high.

"Why are you asking so much for this item?" demanded a curious bidder.

The age-old tempter looked about and speaking out of the side of his mouth, answered, "Discouragement has always been my most useful tool. It is a precious possession. You can see it has had more wear than the others offered for sale. It is used as a wedge to get into a man's mind when all other means fail. With discouragement I can pry open and get inside a man's consciousness and destroy both his spirits and self-confidence."

It is not unusual for men and women to have feelings of insecurity from time to time. In truth, there are few people who are always supremely sure of themselves. The question that each person must answer for himself is— how do my feelings hinder me in my everyday life? Unfortunately, some people fail before they begin. They are assailed by feelings of inferiority.

It is well to remember that there is a world of difference between *being* inferior and *feeling* inferior. Yet, a person who feels inferior for years, often comes to think he is inferior, magnifying his own faults and continually doubting himself.

How much does your self-doubt cost you? How many of the descriptions found below are true of you? Can they be reduced or perhaps be entirely eliminated?

1. You feel you don't do as well as your brother, sister, or friend. When you make comparisons between yourself and others, you always come out in second place with little sense of personal achievement.

2. When something doesn't turn out right, you feel it is

entirely your own fault. You think of many people who could have done it better.

3. You seem to concentrate on an obstacle in your path, and the more you examine it, the more formidable it becomes.

4. You envy those with special skills or talents. You are convinced that you were short-changed at birth. The Almighty did not give you as generous a portion of intelligence as He bestowed upon others.

5. When you are about to accept a new challenge, you keep your mind on how hard it is, how long it will take, and how ill-equipped you are to handle it.

6. You feel defeated before you start something new. Only "status quo" makes you feel at home. You insist on doing the same thing in the same way. You hesitate to start on a new course of action.

7. You put things off till the last minute, then find yourself terribly rushed. Because of the pressure of time, you do a bad job, and prove once again, so you think, that you're just not capable.

8. When people criticize you, it makes you feel insecure and inadequate for a long time. You feel whipped and defeated.

9. You worry about being too short or too tall, too heavy or too slim—you emphasize in your own mind, some physical lack. This inferiority, you feel, is in the way of your progress.

10. You see yourself as an inferior person who will play an inferior role in life.

The above are all poisons! What are the antidotes?

You must think of yourself in positive terms. Few people can think of failure and succeed. Few people catch lions when they think of catching mice. A person cannot make others believe in him if he does not believe in himself.

Give yourself an opportunity to prove you can achieve reasonable success. Break the chain of defeats. Believe in yourself. Stop being baffled. Keep your mind on your work and not on your worry. Worry only succeeds in preventing you from thinking clearly. Failure often comes from a foregone conclusion that you will be a failure.

Establish a schedule for tackling a big job and follow the schedule. Rabbi Chonan of Sepora once illustrated how a difficult task could be made simpler with these words: "The study of the law may be compared to a huge heap of dust that is to be cleared away. The foolish man says, 'It is impossible that I should be able to remove this immense heap, I will not attempt it'; but the wise man says, 'I will remove a little to-day, some tomorrow, and more the day after, and thus in time I shall have removed it all.' "

Yes, a sense of security can be developed in spite of outside calamities, for true security does not lie outside of oneself, but way down deep where a person is assured he is an individual, different from everyone else; that he has a destiny to fulfill, a role to play that no one else can accomplish; that he is a somebody. Therein, lies his true security. In the words of Emily Dickinson,

> "We never know how high we are
> Till we are called to rise;
> And then, if we are true to plan,
> Our statures touch the skies."

Rabbi Jochanan illustrated the same idea with this story: "An apple was hanging from the ceiling. The foolish man says, 'I cannot reach the fruit; it is too high'; but the wise man says, 'It may be readily obtained by placing one step upon another until my arm is brought within reach of it.' "

Man has but one life; he must live it the very best way that he can. He must build a strong, spiritual citadel where sound principles, noble feelings, high aspirations, and lively faith rule. He must practice the tradition of free religious men—that is, he must attempt to advance in wisdom and fortitude; to surmount temporary obstacles with faith and valor; to live by principles of honesty, loyalty, and decency; to take a firm stand against wrongdoing; to remain forever loyal to God through a Torah way of life. He can best serve his cause by developing what is exceptional in him rather than by dwelling upon what is average. An anonymous writer caught this idea when he advised,

> "Bite off more than you can chew;
> Then chew it.
> Plan more work than you can do;
> Then do it."

This then is building security, your security. First become a blessing to yourself that you may be a blessing to others. Know how to be yourself. The confidence you will have in yourself will help you gain the confidence of others. As you think of yourself, so you will be. If the inner you is strong, if you grow to your full stature, then true security is assured for you. In the words of Henry Wadsworth Longfellow,

> "Not in the clamor of the crowded street,
> Not in the shouts and plaudits of the throng,
> But in ourselves are triumph and defeat."

Do you want to succeed? Then to the advice *"know thyself,* and *"behave yourself,"* add, *"believe in yourself."*

CHAPTER SEVEN

Carry Your Own Lantern

I T is important from the point of view of mental hygiene for an individual to think well of himself. A proper self-regard makes it possible for a person to appreciate other people. Respect for oneself is intimately connected with one's capacity for satisfying social relations. Self-esteem is a basic factor in the healthy personality.

Our rabbis always felt that a person must first respect himself before winning the respect of other people. The biblical injunction, "Love thy neighbor as thyself" embodies the fundamental truth that we must love ourselves maturely before we can really love others. The right kind of self-esteem is founded upon accurate self-evaluation and is not to be confused with conceit, which is an over-estimation of one's value. The person who is honest with himself is given neither to false conceit, nor to false modesty, for he has achieved a sense of self-esteem without a feeling of self-importance. It requires a high degree of insight to see ourselves as we really are, and it sometimes calls for a high degree of tolerance for each of us to like the self with which he has to live. The healthy person feels sure of his own worth because he has learned to see himself as others see him. He possesses both self-knowledge and self-acceptance.

What type of person are you? Are you making use of all your talents? Is your biological inheritance paying ample dividends? Do you have confidence in your abilities? Success is built on a mixture of willingness and enthusiasm to take risks. Just as an unused tool becomes rusty from non-use, so a neglected talent withers and dies.

Upon finishing a highly praised concert, Beethoven was surrounded by friends and admirers who could not say enough for his skill at the piano. One woman remarked: "Oh sir, if God had only given me that gift of genius!"

Beethoven looked at the woman for a moment and replied, "It is not genius, madam, nor is it magic. All you have to do is to practice on your piano eight hours a day for forty years and you will be as good as I am. You see, Madam, before I was a genius, I was a drudge."

Daily life is full to bursting with such statements as: "Why doesn't someone tell me these things?" or "If only I could live my life over again!" A fair, though somewhat sharp, retort could be, "Can't you read?" or "Do you ever listen?" or "Where have you been all your life?"

The trouble with some of us is that we study yesterday, think of tomorrow, and miss today. Time is a breeding creature; the minutes propagate hours; the hours beget days; the days raise huge families of months; and before we know it we are crowded out of this life by mere surplus of time's off-spring. The years have turned into decades, and, too often, we have very little to show for the expenditure of time. To a great extent every man is his own ancestor and every man his own heir. He plots his own future and inherits his own past.

Rabbi Meier of Premislan once sadly remarked, "If they will ask me at the Heavenly Court, 'Why were you not like Rabbi Akiva?' I shall not be dismayed, for I will tell them that I do not possess the soul of Rabbi Akiva.

"If they will ask me, 'Why were you not like Rashi?' I shall not be alarmed, for I will tell them that I do not possess the mind of a Rashi. But when they will ask, 'Why

were you not Rabbi Meier?' I shall tremble with fear, for
to myself, I could have been true indeed."

A basic concept that all of us should accept is, "All men
are *not* created equal." The sooner we realize this the happier we will be. Some of us are born with better physical
constitutions and some with greater talents. Literature and
life are filled with examples of such people. We recall that
Keats had weak lungs; Byron had a club-foot; Dostoievsky
was an epileptic; the Kaiser had a withered arm; Steinmetz
had a hunchback. There was no equality in their physical
condition.

We rationalize our lack of industry by pointing out our
lack of talent, and our inheritance of disabilities. But self-
imposed limitations cannot be rationalized. Blindness did
not hamper Milton. Deafness in later life did not deter
Beethoven. Paralysis did not hinder Pasteur. Prolonged
illness did not thwart Robert Louis Stevenson.

How do we feel when a certain person in our social group
outshines us at every gathering? How do we feel when
others are promoted in industry while we remain behind
the filing cabinet or the adding machine? How do we feel
when our neighbor makes a killing on the stock-market,
or has a child prodigy? Do our ulcers act up? Do we curse
our luck? Do we browbeat our mothers and wives? Do we
get drunk, or do we give up and go to sleep?

The spider unreels his web from himself. The men who
make great successes in this world of ours are those who
draw from themselves the structure of their achievement.
They neither imitate nor aim to get from another person
what he has achieved for himself. People fail most frequently when they strive unrealistically for someone else's
goal. The man who succeeds is the person who accepts himself and achieves through his own efforts. He develops
through his own creative work, his own determined think-

ing, concentrating on the tasks before him, spinning his own web, and making the most of his native talents.

A man had a Chinese plate he valued very much. One day it fell and cracked down the middle. Thereupon he ordered six more and to ensure the exact pattern, he sent his broken plate as a copy. When he received the package from China six months later, he was astonished to find the Chinese craftsman had so faithfully followed his copy, that each new plate had a crack right down the middle. It follows that if we imitate others we are bound to follow their imperfections as well. It is more advisable to make our own impression than to be a carbon copy of someone else. It was a wise man who observed, "When a donkey brays, no one pays any attention to him, not even other donkeys. But when a lion brays like a donkey, even the lions in the neighborhood may be pardoned for exhibiting a little surprise."

Of course, an individual gets into serious trouble when he tries to fool himself, to pretend to be something he is not. Many a headache can be avoided by following the simple advice. *"Be yourself!"* If God gave you talent, use it efficiently. Disappointment and failure must result from attempting to convey the impression that you have talents you don't possess. Many a man who thinks he is a dynamo, is only a hand-propelled electric fan.

The wise man does not permit the opinion of others to govern his ideas and his ambition. He knows when to lead and when to follow. He learns to shape his habits so that out of them will develop character, confidence, and happiness.

We are all different and unique. Our differences help determine the type of work we do in this world. We are endowed with specific talents and abilities. The weak seldom become prize-fighters; the blind rarely become pilots; the deaf don't become critics of the opera. However, there are common goals which each man can strive for and achieve. Among these are surely the love of God, the ability to pray, freedom of the mind, the study of man, good scholarship, good habits of work, aesthetic appreciation, love of art, good reading, and constructive use of leisure time. These are among the excellent and enduring values of life. Let us take inventory today!

We should not condemn ourselves for any deficiencies real or imagined, nor despise ourselves if we feel we have failed in life. The craving to achieve a more gratifying and fulfilling life should be appreciated. If we will feel this way, others will too. Then a strange thing will happen. Someone will pay us undivided attention and will show us that he likes to hear our thoughts. He will indicate a genuine interest in us and we will begin to feel worthwhile. We will learn to look at our weaknesses objectively. We will start doing things right which before we had done wrong. We will actually begin to accept ourselves as we really are. That is to say, *we will like ourselves,* even though we are not, and never will be, as gifted as other people. We will find ourselves integrated in our circle. Others will accept us because we have accepted ourselves.

Work with your own talents and be patient. *Proverbs* teaches, "He that is patient is governed with much wisdom: but he that is impatient, exalteth his folly."

When an engineer builds a bridge, he figures on three loads the bridge must bear: the dead load, the live load, and the wind load. The dead load is the weight of the bridge, the live load is the weight of the traffic on the bridge, and the wind load is the pressure of the wind on its super-structure.

This is a parable of life. Life's "dead load" is concerned with managing one's self. Its "live load" is the pressure of daily wear and tear. And its "wind load" is adversity and unalterable circumstances.

The finest furniture, the most exclusive neighborhood, the best of scientific and mechanical genius will not produce a better life. It will take a higher standard of life, rather than a higher standard of living to meet the challenge of this competitive world.

Ideas are liquid assets on our personality balance sheet —the substance of our lives which give meaning to our years. Ideas make us enjoy music, art, a God-made wonder. Our ideas bestow meaning to the book we are reading or the play we are seeing. Ideas give values and a sense of values—the most important elements in human personality. Isn't it true that people who have no values have no value? Isn't it true that some of us neither live to learn, nor have we learned to live?

There is an art to enjoying the blessings of life, and unless we master it, we court unhappiness. We must understand that everything we are and everything we have is a gift from the Creator. Each day we ought to recall the Psalmist's prayer: "O teach us to count our days that we may get us a heart of wisdom."

A young rabbi complained to his master, "During the hours when I am studying I feel filled with light and life, but as soon as I cease to study, the mood disappears. What ought I do?"

Thereupon the elder replied: "It is like a man who journeys through a forest on a dark night, and part of the way is accompanied by a companion who carries a lantern. At length they come to a point where their paths divide, and they must go on alone. If each carries his own lantern, he need fear no darkness."

There are many challenging questions a person might put to himself if he wants to make himself aware of his

aims, goals, and purposes in life. He might turn the search-
light on himself asking,

"If this were my last year on earth, will I be missed?"

"What type of ethical legacy have I left my family?"

"Have I made something of myself, rather than for
myself?"

Character is built just as a building is built—from the
foundation up. If the foundation is shaky, the building will
tilt or collapse. One of our rabbis taught that character, like
a delectable dish, must be achieved with a proper recipe;
of some traits like modesty, man should take a large dose,
and of others like pride, fierceness, cruelty, he should take
but little. Man should weigh the measure of each ingredient.

We may liken our character to an automobile. No matter
what model the car may be, it must travel on a road to
reach its destination, and we must choose that road carefully.

All about us in life there are roads of every kind, leading in every direction. An almost endless network of roads
confronts us—broken roads, highways, upgrade and down,
detours and expressways, mountain ascents and dark forest
trails. But we are the drivers and we are the ones who must
select the road over which we will travel either to self-
attainment or to self-abasement. If we have chosen well,
we need not envy others and feel ashamed of ourselves.

We can appropriate the wisdom of Noah, in Marc Con-
nelly's *The Green Pastures*: "I know I'se not much, but
I'se all I got."

CHAPTER EIGHT

—But No Time to Waste

I·N *Ecclesiastes,* King Solomon says, "To everything there is a season, and a time to every purpose under the heaven." The wisest among men then goes on to enumerate in lengthy detail, "There is a time for birth, a time for death . . . a time to seek, a time to lose. . . " Many of us lose sight of this code for life and spend our years in pursuit of material wealth. Unfortunately, human nature is such that when we allow our eyes to wander over the properties of our fellow men, we desire to be as wealthy, to own as much. From the sunrise of our lives to the very sunset, from early youth to the years of old age, we are embroiled in the battle for wealth, straining forward, completely blind to the permanent damage wrought upon our bodies by our adamant refusal to stop and take stock of our actions. Our hearts keep beating out sacred advice to us, but this is pushed into the background by our all-consuming ambition to accumulate large amounts of monetary assets.

Throughout life, man is periodically made aware that he is but a creation among creations, that the river of his life will some day dry up. *"Time is money"* serves as his guide and motivates his action. The twenty-four hour day seems insufficient for the average person to fulfill his goals. He has made his business, which should be an accessory to the art of living, the primary function of life. He presses ever onward and pretends that his legs do not ache, his body is not tired, his heart is not giving out. He does not understand that he is chasing himself into oblivion. He has forgotten the advice found in *Proverbs,* "Days should speak out . . . years should teach wisdom."

There is a dire need in the world today for sensible goals, for dedication, sacrifice, hard work and dedication to ideals. These values are in direct opposition to the current spirit of our age that caters to security, ease, and mediocrity. Without great dedication and excellent performance in every age, there would have been no great religious or educational leaders, no outstanding scholars, artists, statesmen, scientists, doctors, lawyers, engineers, teachers, and spiritual leaders.

A pupil once asked his rabbi, "I have been wondering why it is that South America, with all its natural advantages, its mines, its rivers and great waterfalls which rival Niagara, is so far behind America."

The rabbi replied after some silence, "I have come to this conclusion. South America was settled by the Spanish who came in search of gold, but North America was settled by the Pilgrims who went there in search of God." This is as true of people as it is of nations. The basic strength of a person is his moral strength. All his productive capacity, all his wealth, cannot save him from ultimate destruction if his moral fiber decays. He sinks into an abyss of material cynicism, indifference to his fellow man, selfishness and greed. In the real sense of the word he is a pauper because he does not treat time as a priceless treasure. He does not understand that each hour represents a new opportunity for aspiration, endeavor, and substance, for adding something to the world's riches and to his own personal growth. The truth is that if "time is money" most people are living beyond their means.

It is common these days to speak of the quest for goals —personal, national, international, and, to some extent, interplanetary. The individual searches for his personal goals. All of life is an anticipation of greener pastures, more exciting days, the fulfillment of dreams, security, and a longer and more adequate life. The young child indicates his great desire to become an adult early in life, by dressing in his parents' clothes. The teen-ager seeks the satisfying companionship of his peer group. The young bride prays for the security of a home. The mother dreams of an adequate life for her children. But the truth is that all of our lives are just about what we, with the help of God, make them, and what we make of our lives reflects the goals we cherish, the values we seek to establish throughout our days.

There is a story that compares our world to a window into which some prankster had broken, and switched the prices on the merchandise. On articles of low value he placed a high price tag, and on the truly precious things and those of sacred value he placed a pitifully low price tag. Observance of people living their twenty-four-hour day will confirm the truth in this story.

It is not uncommon or unnatural for our goals to include a ranch house, a good car, an extended vacation, a comfortable life of security. It is only when this becomes our total goal that there is something wrong. If we believe that these things alone can satisfy us and totally motivate our days we are in real danger, because we then give evidence that we have not learned the difference between living and existing, and that we don't understand that "man does not live by bread alone."

In this race for material wealth, we often sacrifice the very things that money can't buy. It may be good to have money and the things that money can buy, but it is also good to check and make certain that we haven't lost the things that money can never buy. If we are to live happily, we must first understand how to tell and appreciate time: not the hours and minutes, but rather the past, present and future.

Time is infinitely more precious than money. Money can be accumulated, but not time. One minute of time spent can never be regained. Money can be borrowed from those who have a greater supply of it. Time cannot be borrowed as there just isn't enough to go around. An accountant can tell you your exact financial balance, but the amount of remaining time in the bank of life can never be told. There are some people who do not know what to do with their time, as there are people who do not know what to do with their money. There are still others who do not know how to use time or money. "Who ignores time," said Ibn Ezra, "walks in darkness, and who explores it, is illumined by a great light." It is no wonder that King David pleads, "Teach us to number our days that we get us a heart of wisdom."

A man paid a dollar to a miser for a look at his treasures. He stared at the piles of gold, then said, "Now I am as rich as you. All the fun you get from your money is looking at it. You don't use it. Others derive no benefit from it. Of its real value you are really not aware."

It is the quest for life, not for gold, that should motivate people. The Hasidim tell a wonderful story about a rich man who came seeking counsel from the rabbi. Indicating a window which faced the street, the rabbi asked, "What do you see from the window?"

"People," answered the rich man.

The rabbi then led him to a mirror in the room. "And what do you see now?" he asked.

"Now I see myself," answered the rich man.

Then the rabbi said: "Behold, in the window there is a glass, and in the mirror there is a glass. But the glass of the mirror is covered with a little silver, and no sooner is the silver added than you cease to see others but see only yourself."

If a person is interested in himself alone—his needs, his ambitions, his material desires, he cannot be social minded and extend his vision to behold humanity. He should not consider his life a mirror, concerned only with himself, but as a window of a living faith. If we seek personal wealth alone, then the poet who penned these lines might very well be the prophet of the future:

"The atom bomb
Is the final sequel
In which all men
Are cremated equal."

The Chinese tell of a man of Peiping who dreamed of gold, much gold, enough to satisfy his heart's desire. He rose one day, dressed in his finest garments and went to the market place. He stepped directly to the booth of a gold dealer, snatched a bag full of gold coins, and walked calmly away. The officials who arrested him, were puzzled: "Why did you rob the gold dealer in broad daylight," they asked, "and in the presence of so many people?"

"I did not see any people," the man soberly replied. "I saw only gold."

Happiness in life may be thought, sought, or caught, but not bought; happiness and purpose in life is intertwined with the use of time.

Time is a daily miracle. We wake up in the morning and our purse is filled with twenty-four hours of the material of which life is made. It is all ours. It is the most precious of our possessions. No one can take it from us. No one receives more or less than we do. How can time be made to serve us?

We should continue the quest for truth. Only by life-long commitments to truth can we learn truth, embrace it, and love it. Truth makes for security. Truth works for understanding. Falsehood is a sign of cowardice. "The reason we do not see truth is not that we have not read enough books or do not have enough academic degrees, but that we do not have enough courage."

Time should be spent in the love of beauty in its truest forms. We can brighten up the world with music, with poetry, with drama, with literature. We can sing when others remain silent. We can praise when others criticize. The truest expression of the love of beauty is to shun habitually that which cheapens human life, impoverishes human love, and sullies the rich tapestry of a world that mirrors God's perfection.

We must spend time pursuing great moral values, seeking justice, equality, understanding. The Sioux Indians had a prayer, "Great Spirit, help me never to judge another until I have walked two weeks in his moccasins."

Time, without beginning and without end, teaches us respect for tradition and for that which is spiritual, that which transcends the body, its pleasures and its comforts. It is in this spiritual order of our mind and will that we are made in the image of God, and it is in respecting and using these higher qualities to their utmost that we best serve Him, and man too.

Perhaps a person's balance sheet does not indicate great worldly goods. It may be that he cannot write a check for thousands of dollars. This is no cause for genuine worry. There is a burden of care in obtaining wealth, fear in keeping it, temptation in using it, guilt in abusing it. Real security does not come from a large bank balance. It is true that we need many material things. It would be foolish to deny this. But material possessions cannot buy friendship or love. More important than how much a person has or what he has acquired, is what he has enjoyed. He has a priceless store of spiritual possessions. He has a mental treasury of golden memories. He has a mental bankbook of happy events. He has a mental safety vault full of the wisdom of great thinkers. Memory is the mother of imagination; it performs the impossible for man, holds together the past and present, gives continuity and dignity to human life. Memory is the companion, the tutor, the poet, the library, with which a person travels through life.

In the mental vault of wisdom are stored away the solid gold of deep friendships, the untarnished love of children, the many faceted devotion of parents, the precious writings of the ones we love.

Our mental bank-book has so large a balance, that we can draw on it every day without impoverishing ourselves. We should sit down and take stock of all the kind deeds we have done, the unselfish acts we have performed, the happy moments we have given others—the giving of a *gemilas chesed,* the visit to the sick, the comforting words spoken to the depressed. We should think of the bits of happiness we have spread about and the rewards we have received: the smile of a happy youngster, the hand-shake of an old man, a friend's understanding look of gratitude.

Let us draw on the mental treasury of golden memories: memories of happy events, of sitting near a waterfall watching a country stream flow happily over sparkling white rocks, of reclining near a campfire under a star-strewn sky, of walking hand in hand along a scenic country lane, of visiting the family, of playing with nuts on Pesach, of bringing *shalach monos* to friends.

"What endures?" asked the rabbis of old. And in this quaint way they answered their question:

"Rock is strong but iron cleaves it.
Fire melts iron.
Water extinguishes fire.
Clouds come and bear water aloft.
But the winds drive clouds away.
Man may withstand wind.
But fear unmans man.
Wine can dispel fear.
But sleep overcomes wine.
And death sweeps away even sleep.
What then endures?
Only love, love that is deep and genuine."

One of the most exalted prayers in Jewish literature is
the prayer uttered by the Hasidic rabbi Levi Yitzhak of
Berditchev. The love of God dominates his every breath;
he has no thought of asking for wealth. He seeks only to
give service. "Lord of the world," he said, "I do not beg
You to reveal to me the secret of Your ways—I could not
bear it. But show me one thing; show it to me more clearly
and more deeply. Show me what this which is happening
at this very moment, means to me, what it demands of me,
what You, Lord of the world, are telling me by way of it."
With this prayer of the Berditchever Rabbi in our hearts,
we can indeed find everlasting wealth.

CHAPTER NINE

Things That Money Can't Buy

NEVER before have so many of us had it so good. We no longer tremble in fear of hunger. The monotonous burden of killing toil has been lifted from our shoulders. We have inherited freedoms men died for in previous centuries. A shortened work day and week have added hours of leisure time. It would seem that we are living in a dawn of great promise, and that the road to happiness, contentment, and peace of mind that humanity has busily pursued for thousands of years has finally been found.

Yet, ours is a world of unhappiness, tensions, and frustrations. Nuclear annihilation threatens. The fact that twenty-five percent of marriages end in divorce indicates that domestic strife is prevalent. Ten percent of our population, nearly 17 million people, have serious emotional problems, and mental illness has been called the number one disability. The University of Michigan's Survey Research Center recently found that one of every four of us considers his emotional problems serious enough to require professional help. This might account for the $300,000,000 spent annually on tranquilizers.

Something is wrong! Too much desire for material assets? Perhaps! Too much competition? Perhaps! Too much job frustration? Perhaps! Too many family crises? Too much anxiety? Perhaps! Too little faith? Perhaps!

What we need desperately today are hearts capable of bestowing gratitude upon past generations for their experiences and experiments to make this world a better and happier place in which to live—hearts capable of seeing the hand of God in every good deed and in every perfect gift.

What we need today is a modified golden rule which might read: "Live each day as if it were your last. Do every job as if you were the boss. Treat everyone as if he were you." What we need today is people to pray more and curse less; give more and grab less; work more and worry less; love more and hate less; smile more and growl less. If it were so, life would contain more light and less heat. As Albert Schweitzer once observed, "Man does not live in a world of his own; his brothers and sisters are here also." Man should join the great company of those who make the barren places of life fruitful with kindness. He should carry a vision of heaven in his heart, and make the world correspond to that vision. It is never too soon to do a kindness, for no one knows how soon it will be too late.

Unfortunately, one of the easiest things to do is to fill one's life with the second rate, so that the choicest values of life cannot find standing room. One day the artist, William Hunt, was giving instructions to a group of young painters. As the sun went down on a beautiful lake, Hunt noticed that one student was painting an old barn, and had not given attention to the glories of the evening sky. The wise teacher, looking over his pupil's shoulder, finally said, "Son, it won't be light for long. You've got to choose between shingles and sunsets soon. There's time only for one or the other. What is your choice?"

Looking at material values alone is as incorrect a concept of real worth as looking through the wrong end of a telescope. Both inflict injustices to the heavens and to the viewer.

A wealthy business man once offered $4,000 to anyone who could convincingly name four things which money could not buy. He was positive that no one would be able to meet the challenge. He smiled skeptically when one man took out a pad and pencil, wrote four short lines, and passed the note to the challenger. He glanced at it, then gave it a more studied look. Without a word he got out his check-book and made good his promise. The list of the four things money could not buy read:

> A baby's smile
> Youth after it is gone
> The love of a good woman
> Entrance into Heaven

No one can deny that man's needs include food, clothing, shelter, and medical attention. But if he has nothing more than these, a man is on the verge of insolvency and often bankruptcy. He must possess other things as well. There can be no lasting happiness without love. There can be no satisfaction of achievement without work. There can be no release from tension without play. There can be no experience of the joy and peace of life without faith and prayer.

Every one of us can prepare a list of four or more things which cannot be purchased with money, yet can, with effort, be possessed. How many of the following would you include?

Faith

Nothing in the world is more powerful than faith. It is the cement that holds life together. Faith is belief plus will, plus trust, plus work. It is the motivating force behind the world's greatest achievements. One must have faith in God if he is to have faith in himself, in his family, and in his fellow-man. He who believes is strong. He who doubts is weak. Faith is the material that will not shrink when washed in the tears of affliction. Living without faith is like driving a car without lights on a moonless and starless night.

A famous heiress keeps her priceless collection of jewels in the vault of a large bank. One of her prize possessions is a very valuable string of pearls. It is a scientific fact that pearls lose their original luster if not worn once in a while in contact with the human body. So, once a week, a bank secretary, guarded by two plain-clothes men, wears these priceless pearls to lunch. This brief contact with the human body keeps them beautiful and in good condition.

Our faith is a lot like the pearl. It must be used in order to retain its value. It must be worn among the masses of mankind where faith and hope are needed. There is a popular Hebrew saying which should be part of everyone's vocabulary. It is *gam ze l'tova*, whatever happens is for the best. Even if misfortune comes, one should believe that God, in His infinite wisdom and mysterious ways, ordains all for man's benefit. *Gam ze l'tovah* indicates faith. It was expressed by Job, "The Lord hath given and the Lord hath taken away; may the name of the Lord be blessed!"

Peace of Mind

Although we realize the futility of worry, it still remains one of our deadliest enemies. It weakens us physically, is responsible for many of our mental ailments and serves no useful purpose. Yet our peace is shattered by this self-afflicted enemy. Peace of mind is well served with, "The Lord is my light and my salvation; whom shall I fear? The Lord is the stronghold of my life; of whom shall I be afraid?"

Group therapy was once used by a rabbi to help his followers who came to him because their peace of mind was shattered by troubles. When someone came to him with his problems, the rabbi listened attentively and asked him to return on a specified date. On that date, the rabbi arranged to have ten people laden with troubles congregate in his study. When all assembled he excused himself from their midst, telling them he could not listen for the next hour, and suggested that they share their problems with one another. After the hour was up, the rabbi returned. He found them all gone, except for one man who indicated that he had been delegated to remain. He informed the rabbi that after listening to each other's worries, everyone had decided that his personal burdens were not so difficult to bear.

Assuredly, peace of mind cannot be purchased at some bargain counter. It is not for sale. One must weld within himself desire, compassion, love, and faith.

Love

If we were given five minutes' warning before sudden death, every telephone booth would be occupied by people trying to call up others, to stammer that they loved them. Love is the sunshine of the soul. It is more than a sentiment; it is a thirst, a hunger, a need. Love sweetens bitter experience, makes life worthwhile and adds beauty to every life it touches. It gives new hope to the discouraged, new strength to the weak, new joys to the sad. It is not possible to exaggerate the power of love in human relations. If we love, we live. Giving love is just as rewarding as receiving it. It is happiness trolleyed back and forth. A person without love is comparable to an unlit lamp, a motorless car. Perhaps Francis W. Bourdillon gave us the true word picture of love when he wrote:

"The night has a thousand eyes,
 And the day but one,

Yet the light of the bright world dies
With the dying sun.

"The mind has a thousand eyes
And the heart but one,
Yet the light of the whole life dies
When the love is done."

"Love," observed a wise man, "isn't like a reservoir. It can never be drained dry. It's much more like a natural spring. The longer and farther it flows, the stronger and deeper and the clearer it becomes."

Ease of Conscience

Conscience is a walkie-talkie set by which God speaks to His people. A story is told about a party of native bearers in Central Africa who suddenly set down their packs and refused to go forward. When asked for the reason, one said, "Our bodies have gone too quickly for our souls, and we are waiting for our souls to catch up with us." Nothing lies nearer the root of failure to live in peace and harmony than the fact that our spiritual progress has not kept up with our technical progress. Life gives back to us what we put into it; the greater the investment, the greater the return. In reality, all a person needs in life is something worthwhile to do, something or someone to love, and something to hope for. At the pivotal moment between doom or dawn, human values become more precious than material values. In time of disaster, we see with new vividness that material things will not insure our survival.

A little girl was tacking up a new wall calendar, containing the unfamiliar figures of the new year which was about to begin. "It's going to be a beautiful year!" she exclaimed.

Someone who heard the girl's prediction asked, "How

do you know it is going to be a beautiful year? A year is a long time, and you never know what will happen."

"Well," she answered, "a day isn't a long time, I know, and I'm going to take a day at a time, and make it beautiful. Years are only days put together, and I'm going to see that every day in the new year gets something beautiful into it."

"Then," the friend said, "it will be a beautiful year."

CHAPTER TEN

Are You Alive?

PILLS! Pills! Pills!—a billion dollar industry that knows no depression. You have a headache? Take a pill. You wish to lose weight? Will additional pounds make you look more attractive? It really doesn't matter; take the proper pill. Are you too peppy, or too sluggish? You needn't worry. There are pills on the pharmacist's shelf that will solve either difficulty. Does your back hurt? Do your feet burn? Are you constipated? Do you have an itch, suffer from hay-fever, rose-fever, poison-ivy, or tell-tale dandruff? Do you find it difficult falling asleep? Don't fret, medical skill has placed relief in sight. Reach for a pill, then sip some water, and swallow.

Pills! Pills! Pills! There are large ones and small ones. There are colors to fit every taste. Americans are pill-conscious. Less than seven years back, they were credited with washing down 7,000,000 sleeping pills each night. Four years ago, the figure rose to 13,000,000. Two years ago, it hit a high of 22,000,000 pills each evening. Today, men and women gulp approximately 26,000,000 sleep-inducing pills nightly. The search for sleep through pills is followed by days of pill swallowing for relief of headaches and nervous tension. Consumption of aspirins in 1956 hit a high of 11,000,000 a day. The number is much higher now. If you're good with a pencil and paper, try to determine the number of aspirins that would total six or seven tons. This would be the astronomical number of aspirins downed each year.

A mountain of 1,400,000 tranquilizers was gulped down by Americans in 1961.

This shouldn't surprise us, since we live in a world of upside-down values, where the comedian who entertains us is paid most lucratively, and the rabbi and teacher who mold our children's characters are ill-paid. It is a world where the best selling novels are based on a moral structure which we condemn in our private lives; a world where dramas featuring sex, perversion, and lust are box-office hits; a world where we are more concerned with manufacturing death-dealing missiles than with conquering disease.

We live in an age of anxiety. Tension is high. Competition is keen. We compete for love, for money, for prestige, for friends. We are status-seekers and fight for the symbols of our group. We are interested in Dun & Bradstreet ratings, increasing incomes, purchasing new homes, new cars, and new clothing. We are stupified in our pursuit of money. Men of wealth are slaves of desire, and only half satisfied with their possessions. They assume ever greater risks in order to acquire more material wealth. They suffer irritation, frustration, bitterness, and disappointment. The more they possess the more anxiety they feel. The more anxiety they feel the greater the number and variety of pills they add to their diet to prepare themselves to meet the oncoming day. Their insatiable desire consumes all the days of their life.

We have indeed become masters in splitting atoms, developing giant calculators, building mechanical robots, launching satellites, hitting moons, but it seems we cannot find rest for ourselves by day nor sleep by night.

This is no way to live! Life consists of knowing how and what to select of its infinite choice and adjusting ourselves to the selection. If we could learn this lesson, we would not be compelled to swallow pills. We must understand that there isn't enough time to do everything, so we must choose wisely that which will aid best in making our lives count the most. We must be grateful for what we have, and if we can't be thankful for what we receive, we should be thankful for what we escape.

There are pills we can take, sweet-tasting pills that are effective in helping body and soul. Moses offered us life-saving capsules, 613 of them. David condensed them to eleven. Along came Isaiah and reduced them to six. Micah came and cut them down to three. Amos condensed them to two, as it is written, "Thus saith the Lord unto the House of Israel, Seek ye Me, and live." For those who like the "one-a-day" brand, we offer *faith*. Faith extends life. The Bratzlaver Rebbe advises, "The life of a man of faith may alone be called true living. A man of faith has confidence and never descends to despair."

We don't have to reach for a pill. We should reach instead for love, for faith, for knowledge, for friendship. We shouldn't worry about the things that money can buy— these give us aches and pains. We should enjoy the things that money can't buy. We should be thankful for good health. Our sages teach, "There is no wealth, like health." Do we know how to pray? Splendid! Prayers are ladders to Heaven. Can we enjoy the beauties of God's creations, a majestic sunrise, a powerful waterfall, a snow-covered mountain, a walk through the park, the smile of a child, the handclasp of a little boy?

These are effective pills to take. They are not expensive and we can renew the prescription at will. In addition, we will never have to worry as did the would-be-poet who wrote:

> "The stock of pills for varied ills
> Could do with just one more. . . .

One to help me remember
What to take the others for."

What is a healthy life? How shall we use the inheritance of years we receive? Does life consist solely of earning a living, or consuming three meals a day? Living would be empty if it involved only these material aspects of being alive. We are told that Methuselah lived to be 969 years old. Nothing else is told about him. Apparently there is little he did with the quantity of years given him. What good is it to live to be 969, if we don't accomplish much with life's inheritance.

Being alive means being together with people. Being alive means living constructively. Being alive means making use of the ever-decreasing balance of years God has granted us. Being alive means using the talents which are raw materials waiting for man to use them. Thomas Wolfe once wrote, "If a man has a talent and cannot use it, he has failed. If he has a talent and uses half of it, he has partly failed. If he has a talent and has learned to use all of it, he has gloriously succeeded." To know what we have and what to do with it constitutes being alive. The letters of the word A L I V E provide the cue, the prescription for effective living.

The "A" stands for achievement. Life is empty if goals are not achieved. Without worthwhile goals, a person feels inadequate. Of course goals must be realistic. A story is told about a young woodpecker who felt exceedingly chipper one morning. He looked around the forest and decided to start the day by pecking at a huge oak. He had just gotten off to a good start when a bolt of lightning split the tree from top to bottom. The bird hustled out from under the debris, looked up at what was left of the tree, and murmured with a shudder, "Formidable! I didn't even know my own strength." Like the bird, some of us overestimate our abilities and our results. We must understand that genius takes pains, is improved by practice, suffers failures, and only succeeds often after many attempts.

The *"L"* stands for love. We are just not alive without love. It is one of the most precious ingredients in life. It is the fuel that turns the world's motor. It provides motivation for poets, for artists, writers, musicians, and for simple men and women. It brings happiness into homes by creating warmth, understanding, and appreciation. It creates the feeling of being wanted, the satisfaction of belonging. We are taught to love God, love parents, love the House of Worship, love children, love to do deeds of kindness, love one's spouse. When asked what was the most comprehensive rule in the Torah, Rabbi Akiba answered, "Love thy neighbor as thyself."

The *"I"* is important! There are two words in the English language that have exactly the same letters but convey completely different ideas. The words are *united* and *untied*. The "I" placed in the proper place, *unites;* misplaced, *unties*. Few men achieve success by themselves. A great physicist said: "All of Copernicus was in Newton, and all of Newton was in Einstein." Albert Einstein himself said: "Many times a day I realize how much of my own inner and outer life is built on the labors of my fellow men, both living and dead." Helpfulness is the sign of humanity. It is only a Cain who asks, "Am I my brother's keeper?"

The *"V"* stands for virtue. What is virtue? It is the victory of the individual over temptation that assails him. It is the inviting of God into our homes and businesses as well as into our synagogue. It means living in a community for the community. It consists of abiding by the rules of our religious teachings and of society. Lastly, man's virtues are those he lives by, not always those he talks about.

A young man, who was walking with his rabbi, explained that he disliked having to obey. He said, "A fellow hates to have a 'shall' and 'shall not' flung at him every minute. It's so arbitrary."

The rabbi didn't reply. Shortly they came to a sign pointing the way to their destination. The rabbi ignored the sign. The young man exclaimed, "We're going the wrong way! You missed the sign back there." The rabbi calmly replied, "I saw the sign all right, but I thought this looked the better road, and I hate to be told to go this way and that by an arbitrary old sign post." The young man laughed and understood the point.

The *"E"* in *alive* denotes education. One of Judaism's outstanding claims to distinction has been its emphasis on compulsory education. "The scholar," says the Talmud, "takes precedence over the king." In *Leviticus Rabbah* we read, "If you have acquired knowledge, what do you lack? If you lack knowledge, what have you acquired?"

Education is the most valuable legacy parents can leave their children. Spending money for education should not be considered an expense but rather an investment. It awakens a person and makes him deeply aware and appreciative of life. He accepts the world and himself as a growing, changing enterprise. He believes in human rights. The educated man is one whose knowledge matures into wisdom. His life is made meaningful through the never-ending process of learning.

Other forms of relief have been spelled out for us. Enjoying good music, walking along a country road, understanding the purpose of our existence, developing and strengthening ourselves are just a few. Perhaps the simple thoughts of the poet might be read and reread:

"A little more humility seeing our worth is slight;

We are such trivial candles compared to stars at night!
A little more forgiving and swifter to be kind;
A little more desirous the word of praise to find;
The word of praise to utter and a heart rejoice—
A little bit more careful to speak with gentle voice.
A little more true eagerness to understand each other;
A little more real striving to help a shipwrecked brother;
A little more high courage for that which must be done;
These be our resolutions—and God help us everyone!"

These values, followed daily, keep one *alive*. These are remedies which keep us emotionally healthy without need of prescriptions or pills.

CHAPTER ELEVEN

You're Important to Yourself

THERE was a musician who, with utmost care, practiced playing his trumpet many hours each day. Every evening he dressed in his tuxedo, drove to the concert hall, took his place in the orchestra, arranged his music on the stand, and set his instrument carefully upon his knees. But as the music filled the auditorium, he sat motionless, never sounding a single note. The other musicians played. The violins carried the melody through the hall; the oboes, flutes and horns gave depth to the rich composition, and the drums gave it rhythm, but this man with his well-tuned and brightly polished trumpet played nothing. Yet he carefully followed the musical score all the time, never for a single moment taking his eyes off the conductor's baton.

Suddenly the moment for which he prepared had come. He straightened himself, placed his instrument to his lips, and then, the conductor brought him in. Clear and true, a trumpet note rang out—just one note—and no more. Then the man relaxed, his contribution had been made. He had rendered his one note, in time and in tone. When the orchestra leader called for him, he was ready to do what was assigned, and to do his best.

Neither its size nor its importance gives a job its meaning, but rather the part it plays in the overall scheme of things.

"I'm not a bricklayer," claims the man in overalls, "I am a builder of homes and temples."

Of course, it is a privilege to be a great person doing

an important job. But each of us can be great, even though we are not recognized by those about us. The surgeon is important in the hospital, but so is the nurse, the cook, the porter, the elevator operator, the social worker, the dishwasher. Each of them is a great person if he recognizes the importance of what he is doing.

In the museum at Rotterdam is Rembrandt's first painting. It is rough, without marks of genius or skill. It is interesting only in that it shows that Rembrandt began simply and unnoticed. In the same gallery are masterpieces of the same artist. How many years of patient study and practice intervened between these paintings!

It is rather exciting to realize that each of us has a distinctive ability that no person before us, with us, or after us, can display, and that is an exclusive monopoly on our own services. With this knowledge, it is our obligation to develop our God-given talents to the fullest. If we fail, much will be lost. It is true that we may not qualify as another Maimonides, Rashi, or Ramban, or a Mozart, Emerson, Johnson, George Washington or Abraham Lincoln. No! Our purpose for existence may not be something dramatic and noteworthy. But we are expected to make our contribution to mankind, no matter how small and unimportant it may seem to us.

We must remember that time is our most important possession. Time may be said to be lost when it is not devoted to some good, useful purpose, or when opportunities of improvement are neglected. We ought to squeeze the most out of our time, for life is short and uncertain, and the talent we possess should be used.

Work, the use of our talent in the time at our disposal, is the magic lamp that brings us the things we desire. It is the foundation of all prosperity. Instead of wishing for the things we desire, we should work for them. Very few of the tangible rewards we receive in this life offer us lasting satisfaction. Money is spent and fame grows dim, but the personal pride of a job well done neither vanishes nor tarnishes. In the words of Ruskin, "The law of nature is that a certain quantity of work is necessary to produce a certain quantity of good of any kind whatever. If we want knowledge, we must toil for it; if food, we toil for it; and, if pleasure, we must toil for it."

Work is not merely an activity that has to be endured in order to earn a living. There is, and should be, pleasure and satisfaction in what one is doing. The work that we do is an essential part of our lives, not only because by it we earn the necessities of life, but because it gives us purpose and stature.

The Jew is advised over and over again to love work. Far from looking upon manual labor as a curse, the rabbis extolled it as an important factor in man's moral education. Many of the most eminent scholars were manual laborers. Hillel was a wood-cutter; Shammai, a builder; R. Joshua, a blacksmith; R. Chanina, a shoe-maker; R. Huna, a water-carrier; R. Abba, a tailor. They preached that all work is noble that is done nobly.

We may be simple people. Our work may be imperfect and lack beauty. Never mind! Do what you can with what you have where you are today. No person would do anything if he waited until he could do it so well that no one at all would find fault with his work. The poet hopefully advises

"There is some place for you to fill
Some work for you to do
That no one can or ever will
Do quite as well as you."

To be successful, we must put ourselves into our work. We should try to improve yesterday's product by cultivating a keen interest in what we are doing today. In the battle of life it is not the critic who counts; not the man who points out how the strong man stumbled, or where the doer of a deed could have done better. The credit belongs to the man who is actually in the arena; whose face is marred by dust and sweat and blood; who strives valiantly; who errs and falls short again and again because there is no effort without error and shortcoming; who actually strives to do the deeds; who knows great enthusiasm, great devotion, and spends himself in a worthy cause; who, at best, knows in the end the triumph of high achievement; and who, if he fails, at least fails while daring greatly, so that his place shall never be with those cold timid souls who knew neither victory nor defeat.

Chemistry professors are said to have figured that a man's worth is now $32.44 in an inflated market. Dead, lifeless, he may be worth this sum, but alive, man cannot be measured, weighed, and sold for a cash price. His real worth depends on many things. It depends on his services to others, to his family, his community, to mankind itself. It depends on his faith in himself and in others. Surely, no man can be of much worth to anyone who is not first worth something to himself. No person can afford to sell himself short. He must be worth more than the sum total of his chemical properties. He must take stock of his inner values. He must not imitate the simpleton who wrote:

> "I'd be the captain of my soul
>   When life's grim storm clouds thicken,
> I'd be the master of my fate
>   If I were not so chicken."

Our fate, to a great extent, will be what we decide it can be. We must never take our eyes off the goals we have set for ourselves. By concentrating on success, we can be more successful too.

A psychologist of some 20 years experience once confided, "I have talked with, tested, and given vocational counsel to at least 10,000 young men and women. One characteristic that almost all had was the tendency to sell themselves short. We need not worry about the braggart; his kind is not very common. But we do need to worry about the legions of young people who underestimate their ability. When at least three of four sell themselves short, we suffer a community tragedy that is compared to the individual tragedy of an unfulfilled life. It was a wise man who remarked, "I shall pass through this world but once. If there be any good thing I can do, or any talent I can use, let me do it now; let me not defer nor neglect it, for I shall not pass this way again."

CHAPTER TWELVE

Two Unimportant Days of the Week

H E looked up at the doctor with sad, troubled eyes. He was very depressed. His problems were greater than he could handle. "I need help," he pleaded.

"What you need," said the doctor, "is some good entertainment to cheer you up. Why don't you go to the Music Hall tonight? There's a wonderful clown performing there. He's full of life, full of fun—he'll cheer you up for certain."

"But you don't understand, doctor," replied the patient sadly, "I'm the clown."

The art of living is indeed the most important and the most difficult art in the world. If you are ever to live happily, there are certain things you must learn, and certain understandable rules you must follow. To begin with, there are two days in every week about which you should not worry—two days which should be kept free from fear and apprehension. One of these days is yesterday with its mistakes and cares, its faults and blunders, its aches and pains, its frustrations and disappointments.

Yesterday has passed forever. All the wealth in the world cannot bring it back. Beyond asking forgiveness of God and of your fellow man, you cannot undo a single act; you cannot take back a single word spoken. Yesterday is gone forever, never to return. Close the door behind you, so that yesterday's pack of worries do not rush in to destroy today's peace of mind. Refuse to identify yourself with the failures of the past.

The other day that should cause you no worry is tomorrow—tomorrow with its possible adversities, its burdens, its brilliant promise and, perhaps, shabby performance. Tomorrow is beyond your immediate control. Tomorrow has not yet been born. Tomorrow's sun will rise, either in splendor or behind a mass of clouds—but until it does, you have no stake in tomorrow.

Isn't it remarkable that practically all the things you worry about are things that have happened yesterday or may happen tomorrow? Why, then, carry yesterday's troubles, today's problems, and tomorrow's challenges all on your shoulders today? Yesterday's troubles are over. You should have learned from them. Tomorrow's decisions do not yet have to be made. The thought of yesterday's problems and tomorrow's challenges prevents you from functioning today. A distinguished psychiatrist reports that a disturbed patient conceded, "It's easier to lie on a couch digging into the past than it is to sit on a chair facing the present."

If thinking of tomorrow's problems serves as an escape from making decisions today, you are in trouble. Many times you know what you ought to do. You have a sense of duty and responsibility; you have an equal sense of what is right. Your difficulty is not a lack of knowledge but rather a lack of determination. You know what you ought to do, but you lack the inner strength to do it.

To do what you know you should, demands decisiveness, effort, and the willingness to translate a thought into action. That is where your trouble lies. You do not want to be decisive—at least not today. You do not want to make the effort—at least not today. You do not want to translate your thoughts into actions—at least not today. You don't admit that you will never make the effort. You merely deceive yourself by saying that you will make it tomorrow.

So you postpone, delay, rationalize. You give yourself a

dozen reasons why you should wait for tomorrow. However, when tomorrow comes, the same reasons are equally good, and with a sigh of relief you postpone action for another tomorrow. The penalty for all this delay is devastating; it saps effort, weakens your ability to make decisions. On the other hand, the ability to make prompt decisions strengthens your personality.

Whatever you must do, do it now. It won't be any easier tomorrow. Think and act. Strength comes from thought being followed by action.

Today is your day, the only day you have, the day in which you play your part. You may not understand what your part signifies in the great panorama of the universe; but you are here to play it, and now is your time. If you do your best; if you do not magnify troubles; if you look resolutely at things as they really are; if you use your strengths and the blessings which surround you, you will find life a glorious experience.

As you live today, remember that the best thing to give an employer is service; to an opponent extend tolerance; give your heart to a friend; set a good example for your children; give to yourself the priceless heritage of self-respect; and finally give charity and understanding to all men.

The story is told of an ancient king who one night dreamed of great happiness. In the morning he summoned his wisest counselors and demanded that they show him the way to make the dream a reality. Fearing punishment, they offered a formula: "Find a happy man, O King, and wear his shirt. Only then shall thy wish be fulfilled."

The king thought this was excellent advice and sent out an army of searchers to travel the length and breadth of his kingdom for a happy man. They searched for days, months, and years. Their search was fruitless.

After twenty years of searching they were weary and decided to return to their kingdom. On their way home, they came upon a man living alone in a small hut, in the deep forest. He radiated a spirit of outer joy and inner peace. The man was supremely happy, and the searchers sighed with relief. Their search was ended. Then they looked again and knew that they had failed and had wasted twenty years. The man was so poor that he had no shirt.

King Solomon achieved material success, yet he cried: "I gathered me silver and gold and the peculiar treasures of kings and of the provinces . . . the delights of the sons of man; concubines very many. So I was great and increased more than all that were before me in Jerusalem. . . . And whatsoever my eyes desired I kept not from them. . . . And this was my portion from all my labors. Then I looked on all the works that my hands had wrought and on the labor that I had labored to do; and behold, all was vanity and a striving after wind and there was no profit under the sun."

The Talmud poses a searching question: "Who is rich?" And the ready response is: "He who rejoices in his portion." In other words, he who is satisfied with his lot. Or better yet, he who has found his true self, who has achieved his ambition in life.

The aim of life is not to amass large amounts of material wealth, nor is it merely to reach old age. What does living imply? In the words of Robert Louis Stevenson, "To be honest, to be kind, to earn a little, and to spend a little less, to make upon the whole a family happier for his presence, to renounce when that shall be necessary and not to be embittered, to keep a few friends, but without capitulation; above all, on the same condition, to keep friends with himself."

An anonymous writer advises:

"You tell on yourself by the friends you seek,
   by the very manner in which you speak;
   by the way you employ your leisure time,
   by the use you make of dollar and dime.

You tell what you are by the things you wear,
   by the spirit in which your burdens you bear;
   by the kind of things at which you laugh,
   by the records you play on the phonograph.

You tell what you are by the way you walk,
   by the things of which you delight to talk;
   by the manner in which you bear defeat,
   by so simple a thing as how you eat.

By the books you choose from the well-filled shelf—
   in these ways and more you tell on yourself.

So there's really no particle of sense
   in an effort to keep up false pretense."

Forget yesterday's worries and tomorrow's possible anxieties. On the contrary, think positively.

PROMISE YOURSELF

To talk health, happiness and affirmative action to every
   person you meet.

To forget the mistakes of the past and push on to the
   achievements of the future.

To be so secure that nothing can interfere with your peace
   of mind.

To think only of the best, to work only for the best and to
   expect only the best.

To give so much time to the improvement of yourself that
   you have no time to criticize others.

To keep your troubles to yourself; the world is too busy
    to care for your ills and sorrows.

To meet your friends with a smile.

To learn to be yourself.

To learn to enjoy yourself, because it's later than you think.

To try to select a career with wisdom.

To develop enthusiasm—it's the spice of personality.

To learn to be patient.

To attempt to convert your shortcomings into assets.

*Talk health, happiness and affirmative action to every per-
son you meet.*

It's been said over and over again—*worry doesn't solve
anything*. Anxiety never built a bridge, won a battle, or
solved a perplexing problem. The truth is, we render ourselves less useful and much less important if we spend our
time worrying. The best thing to do is to work with all
our strength at whatever opportunities God gives us. A
story is told about a nervous driver who approached an
extremely narrow pass in the Rocky Mountains. He was
frightened at the thought of driving his car along this
narrow road. A sign on the highway reassured him. It
read: *"Oh, yes, you can. Millions have!"*

When we brood over our ills, we magnify them. If a
plank were placed between two roof-tops and an offer of
$10,000 was made to any person crossing from one roof
to another, how many takers would dare the risk? Few,
I think. And of the few who took the chance of crossing,
how many would succeed? Again, the answer would be
few. Yet, if the same plank was placed from one sidewalk
to the next and the same offer was made, uniformed police
would have to keep the lines in order. And of the thousands
who attempted to cross, most would succeed. Why is this
so? Simply, this. In crossing from one roof top to the other,

the people would concentrate on falling. In crossing from one curb to another the fear of falling would not exist.

Think in terms of success and the chances of success are great.

Forget the mistakes of the past and push on to the achievements of the future.

Heraclitus said, "One can never step in the same river twice." The river of life flows on and man changes from day to day. It is futile to brood over past mistakes. Look to the future and prepare yourself for it, so that tomorrow will some day become a yesterday of achievement.

Be so secure that nothing can interfere with your peace of mind.

An Indian fable tells of a mouse who was in constant distress because of its fear of the cat. A magician took pity on it and turned it into a cat. Immediately, it became afraid of the dog. So the magician turned it into a dog. Then it began to fear the tiger. So the magician turned it into a tiger. Immediately it began to fear the hunter. Then the magician said, "Be a mouse again. You have only the heart of a mouse and I cannot help you." Fear, lack of peace of mind, is a destructive force in life.

Think only of the best, work only for the best and expect only the best.

How is this done? Simply—have faith in your objective, have faith in yourself, and have faith in others. Draw a successful plan in your mind and work carefully to achieve it.

Give so much time to the improvement of yourself that you have no time to criticize others.

Before you can improve the next person, you must work

on yourself, and there is so much work you can do here that you should not be able to find the time to criticize others. Remember the words of the unknown poet who wrote:

> "There is so much good in the worst of us,
> And so much bad in the best of us,
> That it ill behooves any of us
> To find fault with the rest of us."

Keep your troubles to yourself: The world is too busy to care for your ills and sorrows. Meet your friends with a smile.

This advice is so valuable. The world is not willing to listen to the constant moaner. The greeting "How are you?" is not an invitation to recite all the woes that have befallen you. Keep your troubles to yourself. Smile. Stop emphasizing your aches and pains. Smile and smile and smile.

Learn to be yourself.

A photographer who aimed to please everybody once advertised:

As you look to me, $1.00
As you think you look, $2.50
As you would like to look, $5.00

Most of us get into one sort of trouble or another because we try to fool ourselves. There is an everlasting temptation to pretend to be something we are not. Many headaches can be avoided by following the simple advice: *"Be yourself!"* If God gave you but one talent, He wants you to use it efficiently. Don't try to impress others with what you don't have. Be smart. Recognize what you don't know. Realize what you can't do.

Learn to enjoy yourself because it's later than you think.
Don't make your life a post-dated check. Don't postpone
living until some distant future date. Don't keep your nose
to the grind-stone day and night. Don't miss the beauties
of God's world by working night and day. However, if
you are tired of living you might follow these simple rules:

1. Remember there is nothing more important than your
   job. It comes first and always. Be at the office daily
   and on Saturday and holidays.
2. Take your work home with you. Worry about it. Worry
   your family about it. Pace the floor at night. Look at
   the pessimistic side only.
3. Never, but never, take a vacation. Postpone it. Say you
   just can't spare the time. If you are forced away, cut
   your vacation short and worry all the way home.
4. Never delegate responsibility. Do all the jobs yourself.
   No one can do it as well as you. All jobs need your
   personal attention.
5. Try to outdo your younger colleagues in every phase of
   work.
6. Never relax when you eat. Answer the telephone, write
   on the table cloth, keep your mind on your work.
7. Jump up from each meal as soon as the last bite has
   been swallowed.
8. Don't spend any time with your children. Wait until
   you retire from business to get to know them.
9. Never say "No" to any social or business request.
10. Eliminate reading, resting, relaxing. They are all time
    wasters.

Keep this up and you will have loads of time—but you
won't know it.

Try to select a career with wisdom.
A little watch, dissatisfied with being in a pocket, envied

Big Ben, the great tower clock. "I wish I could be up there," said the little watch. "I could then serve the multitude." And suddenly the little watch had its wish granted. It was drawn up to the tower. But from below it was invisible. Its elevation had become its annihilation.

Develop enthusiasm—it's the spice of personality.

It's contagious. It is the very air of a functioning person; the sign of a large and active mind. It gets things done. It's like high octane gas. It's working on 8 cylinders instead of four. It's the oil in the engine, the grease in the wheels.

The great industrialist, Charles Schwab, was noted especially as an executive who secured amazing cooperation from the people who worked with him and from those with whom he had business relations. When he was asked what he considered the prime ingredient in his character that had helped make him such a towering success, he answered, "I consider my ability to arouse enthusiasm among people the greatest asset I possess."

No man ever became eminent in any phase of life who did not have in his makeup a very considerable element of enthusiasm. Something more is needed than dull plodding work.

Learn to be patient.

Three hundred years ago a prisoner condemned to the Tower of London carved on the wall of his cell this sentiment to keep up his spirits during his long imprisonment: "It is not adversity that kills, but the impatience with which we bear adversity." Rebelling against difficulties that cannot be immediately avoided only makes a bad situation worse. Once you recognize that time cannot be rushed and that "riding out the storm" is your best course of action, your life will be easier. "O Lord," prayed a young man, "give me the power to bear patiently what must be borne."

Attempt to convert your shortcomings into assets.

Can you picture Angelo Siciliano, 47 years of age, pulling 72 tons of steel along a track? At 16, he was pale and a "97 pound runt," nervous and a prey to bullies. Today he is called Charles Atlas.

Gertrude Klasen was born in the slums of London. She had anything but a good beginning. But Gertrude had made up her mind to succeed. She wanted to get into the theatre. A dramatic coach assured her that, though she might learn to look and act like a lady, with her raucous voice and cockney accent she'd never fool anyone. That was all Gertie needed. From being wishful she became determined. You may have seen this same Gertie in George Bernard Shaw's *Pygmalion* on Broadway, in the role of Eliza Doolittle, the flower girl who, in a flood of cockney, bawls out a lady for the rude behavior of her son.

Gertrude Klasen became Gertrude Lawrence, who is a dashing figure in international society. From poverty she achieved wealth, from commonness, good breeding. For cockney speech, she substituted exquisitive diction. With no formal education she became a guest professor at Columbia University. She was motivated by being born on the wrong side of the tracks.

There are many people who have turned their liabilities into assets. Beethoven is a startling example. Afflicted from childhood with an organic hearing deficiency, at 28 he was already quite deaf. Four years later he could barely hear a full orchestra without the aid of an ear trumpet. That was the year he composed his wonderful "Second Symphony," which was later to be surpassed, as his deafness became more acute, by the "Eroica," the "Moonlight Sonata," the "Fifth Symphony," and finally after he had been completely deaf for 25 years, his glorious "Ninth Symphony."

There was a backwoodsman who was uneducated, ungainly, and almost strikingly ugly. His birth was lowly, his mother being an illegitimate child. All his life he remained aware of his social shortcomings. No person could have started lower, or risen higher. Abraham Lincoln became the President of the United States. He compensated for his liabilities by using his great qualities of mind and heart to rise above them. He worked desperately hard to overcome his initial handicap.

Darwin, Heine, Keats, Stevenson, Pope, Parkman, Kant, Byron, Chopin, Wagner, Bacon, Aristotle, Dostoevski, Socrates, Voltaire—all developed extraordinary abilities despite their poor beginnings.

All these famous men succeeded because they were compensating for some inferiority. Alfred Adler once said that no one succeeds without an inferiority complex. Facing their own inadequacies, they were determined to alter their lot.

Each one of us possesses personal liabilities. Each one of us has some organic weakness. What we must do is to take note of our weakness and to overcome it. Others have done so. Why can't we?

There is an old legend about a fisherman, who lived on the banks of a river. Walking home with his eyes half-closed one evening after a hard day's toil, he was dreaming of what he would do when he became rich. Suddenly his feet struck against a leather pouch filled with what seemed to him small stones. Absentmindedly he picked up the pouch and began throwing the pebbles into the water.

"When I am rich," he said to himself, "I'll have a large

house." And he threw a stone. He threw another and thought, "I'll have servants and wine and rich food."

This went on until only one stone was left. As the fisherman held it in his hand, a ray of light caught it and made it sparkle. He realized then that it was a valuable gem, that he had been throwing away the real riches in his hand while he dreamed idly of unreal riches in the future.

You hold in your hand the power to enrich your life. Some time ago, the Metropolitan Museum of Art held a display of contemporary art at which $52,000 was awarded to American sculptors, painters, and artists in allied fields. The award for the best painting went to an Illinois artist. His canvas was described as "a macabre, detailed work showing a closed door bearing a funeral wreath." Equally striking was the work's title: *That which I should have done, I did not do.*

Perhaps you cannot win an award for painting. You might not even be willing to attempt to produce a work of art. Yet there are so many things in life that you would do, you say, "if only there were time."

The years slip by and with them opportunities for serving others, for doing good personally. Each day presents you with thousands of opportunities for reaching out to the world as far as you can. You have only to grasp the chance.

Any day is a good day to begin, especially today!

CHAPTER THIRTEEN

Only You Can Make Yourself Unhappy

THREE friends agreed that they would separate, and each would master a particular field of learning by going to a special school. After a set time, they were to meet and relate their experiences. When they met one had perfected a telescope through which he could see what was happening in distant lands. The second had perfected a vehicle that could cover great distances in the briefest time. The third had prepared a tonic that could destroy all disease.

As the first friend was demonstrating his telescope, he saw a distant city terribly distressed because the king's daughter was critically ill and no physician could cure her.

Said the second friend: "Hop into my speed carriage and let us go to help her!"

Said the third friend: "Take me along. I have the perfect tonic."

In minutes they were at the city. The tonic was given and the princess soon recovered. The king had promised his daughter to the person who saved her life.

Said the first friend: "She is mine. I saw her in my telescope."

Said the second friend: "She is mine. My carriage brought us here."

Said the third friend: "She is mine. My tonic saved her life."

The king asked his daughter to decide who was entitled to her hand.

She reflected for a while and answered: "You have all

had a hand in saving my life. But I do want to look into the future. What will serve my welfare best? It won't be the telescope nor will it be the carriage. Only the tonic can best serve me and so I will marry the person who perfected the health-giving medicine."

The insight offered in this interesting story can be applied to our own lives. What is the most precious ingredient in life? What makes for a happy life? How can we decrease the amount of unhappiness so many of us experience? How can we make our lives meaningful and adequate?

A wise man once pasted the following in his hat as a reminder along the way of life: "*Any man can spoil himself for himself.*" He can make his life worthwhile or he can make it merely a matter of existing for a certain number of years. He can make it productive or a void.

The tragedy of life is what dies inside a man while he still lives. He murders genuine feeling, spontaneity, awareness of other people. He forgets how to give of himself. He imprisons the values that yield happiness, contentment, and productivity. The tragic actors of life are those who drift and never discover that life has begun; for them, the curtain never rises. A person cannot *find* life worth living. He must *make* it worth living. A good prayer might be: "*O Lord keep me alive while I am still living.*"

Happiness is not a matter of position in life but of disposition. Man has it within his power to make himself happy or unhappy. An ancient king once offered this bit of advice to the people in his kingdom:

Be not too wise, nor too foolish
Be not too conceited, nor diffident,
Be not too haughty, nor too humble,
Be not too talkative, nor too silent,

Be not too hard, nor too feeble.
If you be too wise, men will expect too much of you.
If you be too foolish, you will be deceived;
If you be too conceited, you will be thought difficult;
If you be too humble, you will be without honor;
If you be too talkative, you will not be heeded;
If you be too silent, you will not be regarded;
If you be too hard, you will be broken;
If you be too feeble, you will be crushed.

One of the great arts in living is to learn the art of accurately appraising values. Everything that we think, that we do, that we have given to us, that in any way touches our consciousness, has its own value. These values are apt to change with one's mood, with time, or because of circumstances. We cannot safely tie ourselves to any material value, for the value of all material possessions changes continually, sometimes overnight, and has no permanent, set value. The only real values are those of the spirit. They remain with us, giving us happiness and enrichment. A wise man once said, "To have what you want is riches; but to be able to do without is power."

Life is very much like a mirror. Smile into it and it will smile back. Frown at it and it will frown back. No person ever makes us angry; we grow angry as a result of our own choice.

Are you making yourself unhappy? You may be bringing unhappiness into your life if:

You allow yourself to grow so sensitive that you live in constant pain!

Learn how to accept criticism. The entire world isn't trying to find fault with you. Criticism should leave you with the feeling that you have been helped. After all, the largest room in the world is the room for improvement. Sensitivity may indicate a feeling of inadequacy, which in turn makes you vulnerable to pain and anguish. Sensitivity leads to anger, and anger is only one letter short of danger.

You nurse your grudges until they are an intolerable burden!

A mother once cured two grown children of constant griping. She ordered them to clean all the windows in the house, but both had to do this chore at one window—one inside, one outside. They started with a growl—but ended in laughter. It is easy to give another a "piece of your mind"; but when you are through, you have lost your own peace of mind.

A better tonic would be to pray more and curse less; give more and grab less; work more and worry less; love more and hate less; smile more and grumble less. If you do this, your actions would have more light and less heat.

Learn to smile. It sets the day straight.
Learn to laugh. It's better than medicine.
Learn to have faith. It helps in moments of sadness.
Learn to forgive and forget. It decreases mental anguish.

The poet wisely cautions:

"That man may last, but never lives,
Who much receives, but nothing gives:
Whom none can love, whom none can thank,
Creation's blot, creation's blank."

You can imagine troubles until they are real!

We look old because we remember the weight of the burden of last year's experiences and flounder around in the sea of next year's worries. Rather than by lifting our faces, we grow young by lifting our thoughts. It is the mind, not the physical body, which bears the stamp of age and reflects it in the body. Don't borrow trouble; the interest on the loan will break you.

Why think of trouble? Instead of getting mired in this bit of quicksand, hang on the walls of your mind the memory of your successes. Inventory your strengths, not your weaknesses. Think of the good jobs you have done, instead of the number of failures you have met. Think of the big moments in your life instead of the tragic ones. Blessed is the man who is too busy to worry in the daytime and too sleepy to worry at night.

Much mental turmoil comes from trying to live all of life at once. You lump all past worries and future problems together and take them on all at once—now. Remember that yesterday is a canceled check. Tomorrow is a promissory note. Today is ready cash. Spend it wisely.

You can become so wrapped up in yourself that you become very small!

A man who had been attending services every Shabbos suddenly stopped coming to the synagogue. When the rabbi inquired about this, the congregant said he felt he could accomplish just as much remaining in the comfort of his home and praying by himself.

One evening the rabbi decided to visit his errant congregant. He found the man seated comfortably at the fireplace reading a book. The rabbi, without a word, sat down near the host. He then took a live piece of coal with the tongs and set it in a corner of the fireplace. While the rest of the fire was warm and glowing, the isolated piece of coal grew paler and paler until it was cold and dead. The rabbi said nothing. Next Saturday, the man was back in his usual place at *shul*. He had learned the lesson well— that no man or woman ever makes it alone.

The "I" must be given its proper place in life. An unknown author indicated the needs of the world when he wrote:—

"A little more kindness and a little less creed,
A little more giving and a little less greed;
A little more smile and a little less groan,
A little less kicking a man when he's down;
A little more "we" and a little less "I"
A little more laugh and a little less cry;
A few more flowers on the pathway of life,
And fewer on graves at the end of the strife."

Instead of being envious of the next person's good fortune, get out and collect the living you believe the world owes you. Fiske hinted at this when he wrote:

"I AM—the power of self knowledge.
I THINK—the power to investigate.
I KNOW—the power to master facts.
I FEEL—the power to appreciate, to value, to love.
I SEE—the power of insight and imagination.
I BELIEVE—the power of faith.
I CAN—the power to act and accomplish.
I OUGHT—the power of conscience.
I WILL—the power to do.
I SERVE—the power to be useful."

It might be well to remember

"I am only one, but I am one.
I cannot do everything, but I can do something.
What I can do, I ought to do;

And what I ought to do, by the grace of God
I will do."

*You can become so envious that you cannot enjoy what you
have!*

The other fellow's grass looks greener. Envy is quicksand and often fatal. The more you indulge, the deeper in
you get.

Only you can make yourself unhappy!

You can hold many people under suspicion until no one
believes in you. You can insult your friends until you have
no friends left.

Do you want friends? Be friendly.

Do you want justice? Be fair with others.

Do you want consideration? Be considerate yourself.

Do you want courtesy? Be courteous.

A rabbi was asked for the secret that gained him a
happy, peaceful old age. He replied, "I never cherished
anger with my family; I never envied those greater than
myself, and I never rejoiced in the downfall of another."

Edward Markham, in one of his poems, tells about an
old philosopher who was sitting under the shade of a tree.
A man approached and asked, "What type of people live
in yonder town? I want to move into it."

The old philosopher looked at the man and asked, "What
type of people live in the town you are planning to leave?"

"Ah," answered the man, "in the town I wish to leave
live cold, dishonest, unfriendly, selfish people."

"Do not move into this town," replied the philosopher.
"The same people live here as well."

No sooner had the stranger left, when a **second** man

appeared and made the same inquiry, "What type of people live in yonder town?"

Again the old philosopher asked, "What type of people live in the town you plan to leave?"

"I hate to leave my town," answered the second man. "It is filled with warm, friendly, hospitable people."

The philosopher looked at the man and quickly replied, "Don't fret for a single minute. You can move into this town. The same people live here as well."

A passerby had heard both questions and both answers. Said he to the philosopher, "How can you give two different answers to identical questions?"

"It's really simple," he replied. "The person who finds liars in one town will find them in another. The person who finds warmth, friendship, and honesty will find it anywhere he lives."

What are you looking for in life?

CHAPTER FOURTEEN

Man's Quest for God

A STORY is related about a youngster playing hide-and-seek with his friends. For some unknown reason they stopped playing when it was his turn to hide. When he learned what had happened he broke into tears. His old grandfather came out of the house to see what was troubling him and to comfort him.

"Do not weep, child," he coaxed, "because your friends left and did not come to find you. Perhaps you can learn a lesson from this disappointment. All of life is like a game between God and man. But it is God who weeps, because man does not play the game fairly. God is waiting to be found and man has gone off to search after other things."

God is always waiting to be found, but He must be sought with sincerity, faith, and honesty. He is never so busy with the affairs of the universe that He is not concerned to be with and help every individual who turns to Him.

Man must be willing to serve God and not constantly demand that God serve him. Too often a person is tempted to use God when he ought to be used by God. He must be willing to submit to His will.

"Seek ye the Lord while He may be found," cried Isaiah. "Call ye upon Him while He is near." Look for God not for His gifts. The rabbis tell us, "Let a man love God with a perfect love whether it go well with him or ill."

True belief means finding God and filling your life with His spirit, learning to understand His commandments, and to follow His path. What roots are to a tree, faith is to the individual. Great oak trees have great roots. Great souls have great faith. The secure man has that intangible confidence in himself, in his capacities to be and to do, and a recognition of God who may transform and enrich his life.

The Rabbi of Kitsk once asked a number of learned men, "Where is the dwelling of God?" They were shocked at the question. "What a thing to ask? Is not the whole world full of His glory?" they replied. The pious scholar thought for a moment, and then quietly answered his own question: "Where is God? God dwells wherever man lets Him in."

A state ambassador once spent a sleepless night through anxiety over the problems that had faced him the previous day. It seemed that he could do nothing about them—except worry. His old servant said to him, "Sir, did God govern the world before you came into it?" "Undoubtedly," replied the ambassador. "And will He rule the world when you have gone out of it?" "Of course He will." "Then, sir, can you trust Him to rule the world well while you are in it?" The ambassador sensed the lesson that was being taught him and soon relaxed sufficiently to go to sleep.

When Rabbi Yitzchak Meir was a youngster, his mother once took him to see the Maggid of Koznitz. There someone said to him: "Yitzhak Meir, I'll give you a gulden if you can tell me where God lives!" Looking directly at his questioner, he replied: "And I'll give you two gulden if you tell me where He doesn't."

Several years ago, a tourist visited a new hydroelectric development on the Niagara River. The guide explained it all, pointing out that there were 16 giant turbines to produce electrical current from the rushing waters. Then he informed the visitor there were more than 400 million separate pieces in the giant machines and in the power plant. The startling thing was his next statement: "The resident engineer knows where every piece goes and what it is supposed to do!" "If an electrical engineer could know all that," thought the visitor, "why should we be surprised that God knows all about us." The same thought occurred to a rabbi who wished to help a confused congregant.

"Do you really believe the Bible story about the parting of the Red Sea for Moses and the Jews?" asked the congregant.

The rabbi smiled for a moment and replied, "I certainly do. If DeMille can do it, God can do it too!"

"What can we wish for in a heritage that is not to be found in God?" asks author Sinclair Lewis. And he answers the query with these words. "Would we have large possessions? He is immensity. Would we have a sure estate? He is immutability. Would we have a term of long continuance? He is eternity itself."

Every day, whatever you do, wherever you go, God goes with you. You are surrounded by His protecting presence. It isn't difficult to realize that beyond yourself there is a power at work for you, and that though that power is greater than you, it is also within you, ever available for your health and peace. You need only understand that to hear the call of God, you must be within listening distance. If you have a faith, however dim, which makes sense out of life, and gives meaning to your fleeting days, and dares to believe the best in the face of the worst the years can do —do not let it go. A young girl, her homework not fully prepared, got up to recite Psalm 23 in her religious class. She didn't recite the psalm as most of us know it, but what she said made real sense. "The Lord is my Shepherd; that's all I want."

An unknown poet captured the essence of deep faith when he wrote:

> Where there is love
> There must be faith;
> And where there is faith
> There is peace indeed;
> Where there is peace,
> There must be God—
> And where there is God
> There is no need.

A young child once taught the significance of faith to her mother. Both mother and daughter were preparing to retire for the night, and both were a bit frightened of the darkness. After the lights were extinguished, the child caught a glimpse of the moon outside the window. "Mother," she whispered, "is the moon God's light?" "Yes," replied the mother, "God's lights are always shining." The young child was silent for a moment and then asked, "Will God blow out His lights and go to sleep?" "No, my child," replied the mother, "God never goes to sleep." "Well, so long as God is awake I am not afraid," said the child.

A man once prayed:

> "Grant me, O God, Thy merciful protection;
> And in protection give me strength, I pray;
> And in my strength, O grant me discretion;
> And in discretion make me ever just;
> And with my justice may I mingle love,
> And with my love, O God, the love of Thee;
> And with the love of Thee the love of all."

If only man feared God as much as he fears man! If only man tried to impress God as much as he tries to impress man. The Talmud relates a story about Rabbi

Jochanan ben Zakkai. This saintly teacher lay on his death-bed, laboriously breathing away his last few moments on earth. His grief-stricken disciples begged him to impart one final word of wisdom, before eternity forever sealed his lips.

With great effort, straining every fiber in his tortured body, he whispered, "May your fear of God be as great as your fear of man." His students were astonished at this message. "Master, you must mean the contrary: Our fear of man should become as great as our fear of God."

"No, my sons," the Rabbi sighed with a dying gasp. "Thinking that God does not see you or, in His love, will not punish you, you are less fearful of doing wrong in His eyes than in the eyes of your fellow man, who, you suspect, may find you out and have you punished under his law." There is a great deal of insight in Rabbi Yochanan's observation that man is more concerned with the fear of man than he is with the fear of God.

The Hasidic rabbis ask: Why do the prayer book and the Scriptures refer to "the God of Abraham, the God of Isaac, and the God of Jacob?" Why is God repeated each time? And they answer that it is to teach us that the God of Abraham was not the same as the God of Isaac, and the God of Isaac was not the same as the God of Jacob. Each generation grows in its knowledge of God. Every individual sees God in his own way. The *Midrash* teaches: God comes to each one according to his strength. For know thou, if God had come upon Israel with the full might of His strength when He gave them the Torah, they would not have been able to withstand it, as it says: "If we hear the voice of the Lord our God any more then we shall die!" God, however, came upon them according to their individual strength.

There are two books which should be kept in every home and should be read by every member of the family: the

Bible, which tells of the miracles of God, and the seed catalogue, which proves them. Dr. Charles M. Crowe once listed the contributions made in the production of 100 bushels of corn on one acre of land. "Man," he said, "contributed labor. God contributed a few things, too: 4 million lbs. of water, 6800 lbs. of oxygen, 5200 lbs. of carbon, 1900 lbs. of carbon dioxide, 160 lbs. of nitrogen, 125 lbs. of potassium, 40 lbs. of phosphorus, 75 lbs. of yellow sulphur, 50 lbs. of magnesium, 50 lbs. of calcium, 2 lbs. of iron, and smaller amounts of iodine, zinc, copper, and other things. . . . One hundred bushels of corn! Who made them grow?"

An old rabbi, centuries ago, asked the question, "We are told, thou shalt love the Lord thy God with all thy heart, with all thy soul, and with all thy might. How can we love God when we cannot see Him? He is the invisible Spirit, the intangible Mind of the Universe." And the answer to the question was, "We can love God best by loving His letters best! . . . How does a child learn the alphabet. He learns one letter at a time—A, B, C, D, E, F—and then he combines the letters into words, and then the words into sentences, and finally he can read a book." The ancient rabbi said: "Every person is but one letter in God's book. The more letters you come to treasure, the more you can love God."

Belief in God can work miracles—the miracle of changing a personality, of developing faith, building courage, strengthening moral self control, striving for an ideal, of believing. God makes a promise. Faith believes it. Hope anticipates it. Patience quietly sees it fulfilled. God's promises, however, do not all mature in 90 days.

Two boys were conversing about Elijah's ascent to heaven in the chariot of fire. Said one, "Wouldn't you be afraid to ride in such a chariot?"

"No," was the immediate reply, "not if God drove."

CHAPTER FIFTEEN

Love and Marriage

MANY married couples seem to be at odds too soon after saying, "I do." In the United States today, one out of four marriages ends in divorce. The majority of these husbands and wives seek divorce mainly because their marriages have not lived up to their expectations. They are bored, disappointed, or no longer in love. They do not understand each other, and unfortunately when they finally do, they are no longer interested. The wife didn't get what she was expecting and the husband didn't expect what he was getting. The wife claims she just isn't understood and the husband claims she just doesn't understand. The wife states that he doesn't listen and the husband states that she talks too much.

Ask the freshman in high school, "Son, do you understand love?" He will write an essay. Ask the old bachelor. He will write a book. Ask the married man. He just grins and shakes his head. He has learned that while love and marriage go together, it isn't quite the love that has been portrayed on his 21″ color television screen. He knows that it takes two to be in love, and it takes both mates to make marriage work. In *Sotah*, we learn, "Mating is as hard as the cleaving of the waters of the Red Sea."

Our rabbis, with their deep insight into human nature, understood the meaning of love in marriage. "Serve those who love you and those near unto you with your person and your substance," advises Maimonides. If you truly love, you give the most precious thing you have—yourself. You

give of your life, your time, your joy, and your interest.
You give knowledge, confidence, and understanding. *Perek*
wisely comments, "Whenever love depends upon some material cause, with the passing away of that cause, the love
too passes away, but if it be not dependent upon such a
cause, it will last forever." It is interesting to note the
order of Isaac's meeting with Rebecca. "He took her, he married her, he loved her." The *Chumash* teaches that his love
existed not only before marriage but after it as well.

Unfortunately, today, many people who marry do not
understand what love is. They believe that love is a for-
tuitous accident which occurs when people chance to meet
and immediately feel the magnetism of infatuation. The
lucky pair, so the fable goes, meet, marry, and live happily
ever after. This wishful thinking is founded upon fantastic
assumptions popularized by love stories, songs, movies and
television, and the absorption of this sentimental hogwash
prepares one for a marriage of disappointment and frustration. The person who claims he is married for twenty-
five years without a single cross word having passed
between the marital partners shows evidence of a poor
memory, or indicates that his marriage partnership is an
association of two spineless people. The course of true
love never runs smoothly. Abraham and Sarah had their
problems. Jacob's marital life was filled with problems that
could wreck a marriage today.

It is impossible to exaggerate the power of love in
human affairs. The keystone of living, it makes light of
everything that is heavy, for it bears the burden without
being burdened, and makes sweet and tasteful everything
that is bitter. Love is the answer to our deepest needs as
human beings. "It is not good for man to live alone," is a
bit of wisdom from Genesis. Love represents the faith a
person has in another's potentialities. It is the active power

that breaks through the walls which separate us from each other. It is a moving, a growing, and a working together.

To love is an art. To experience it, you must work at it first, as you would at any other art, such as music, painting, carpentry, sewing, or cooking. To master an art, you must feel, at that time, that nothing else in the world is more important. This is why so many people, in spite of a deep-seated craving for love, fail to achieve it. Too much energy is spent learning how to achieve success, prestige, money, power, or popularity, and practically no time is devoted to learning the art of love.

Do you want to be an expert at this most important function in life? You do? Then practice it; and to practice an art you must follow certain requirements. The first is discipline. You must work at love in a disciplined way. It is essential that you concentrate. You must live fully in the present; focus on the here and now. People who love each other do not spend all of their leisure time at the TV set, the movies, or with their next door neighbor.

Be patient; you cannot learn any art if you are after quick results. There may be instant tea, instant coffee, instant mashed potatoes, but there just isn't any instant love. To master this art, you must devote your entire life to it.

A marriage counselor challenged a bickering couple. "Suppose you were digging for oil and went down only 300 feet. Would you give up? Would you give up if you thought that by digging another 100 feet, you might strike a gusher?" Generous returns in marriage can be anticipated with persistent and patient cultivation.

The catered affair, the hundreds of dollars worth of fresh roses, and the expensive wedding band, do not insure marital happiness because a successful marriage consists of more than a prayer-book, a check-book, and a cook-book. It is a result of blending ideas, interests, and personalities.

A happy marriage is not a gift, and involves more than finding the right person. It is *being* the right person.

Pre-marital and marital counseling makes up a good deal of our religious literature. The Talmud teaches man about women: "Ten measures of speech descended to the world; women took nine and men one. . . . If a man wants to give his wife pleasure, let him clothe her in linen garments. . . . Women are light-minded." The other side of the picture can also be found. "God endowed woman with more intelligence than man. . . . A woman spins even while she talks. . . . Women are compassionate."

A writer describing the fair sex once stated, "The Lord took the finest materials in his possession; the white of lilies for cheeks, the red of coral for lips, the blue of heaven for eyes, the black of ravens for hair; added the grace of loveliness, kindness, and tenderness, mixed all these ingredients together and out of it came forth women." With these raw materials, it would seem that only the best finished product would result.

Of course, marriage is a two way proposition and in our holy writings there is a statement which teaches, "A man gets the wife he deserves." If he has an unhappy marriage, he might look for a good number of the reasons in his own actions. Yet, we ought to determine what wives can do to insure marital happiness, since they are the stronger of the two sexes.

E. Gilmour Smith said, "Two pieces of iron which are joined by plates and bolts may be disconnected easily, and each separate piece remains the same as it was before. But when welding has been used to join them, the metal of each flows into and becomes a part of the other. No longer are they two separate pieces, but have become one. Perhaps the importance attached to marriage can be found in a quote from the Zohar, "God creates new worlds constantly. In what way? By causing marriages to take place."

In Proverbs we read, "Every wise woman builds her house, but the foolish woman plucks it down with her own hands." She can do this by listening to gossip about her spouse, by withholding herself, by failing to confide, to listen, and to share. A man will soon understand that "It is better to dwell in an attic nook than in a house together with a contentious woman."

The following recipe for wrecking a marriage may be given to wives:

Begin by attacking his pride. Snicker at his ambition. Belittle his plans. Laugh at his ideas. Call him a dreamer, a big-time nobody who majors in failure. If any of his plans succeed, call it fool's luck and minimize its importance and results. Display a lack of respect for him. If he calls on the phone, begin by telling him that he interrupted your work. Tell him you are in a hurry and can't waste time. Ask him in "business-like tones" what his purpose is in calling, and remind him firmly that evidently you don't have the same leisure he enjoys. Show him in every way that you are smarter than he is. Tell him that everything he does is wrong and that you could have handled it better. Warn him against doing anything without first consulting you. Tell him he is clumsy and has two left feet.

When he arrives home from work, be certain to greet him with a tired look, uncombed hair, torn shoes, a mop in one hand, a pail of dirty water in the other, and a flood of words. Immediately, send him on errands; to the grocer, to the fruit store, to the incinerator, to bring junior home from a friend's house, to give mother a lift to the bus station. Complain about the children, the household chores, his lack of understanding. Point out all his imperfections, and remind him that it is really your own fault because your

parents tried to warn you about marrying him. Compare
him, unfavorably of course, to your former suitors, especially those who happen to be in a better financial position.
Remind him that you could have had mink, diamonds, maids,
all the luxuries of life, had you married Yankel, Irving,
Herman, or any of the many men who pursued you and
pleaded for your hand.

On the other hand, what does a wife want out of
married life?

She wants to be accepted socially. She wants to feel she
belongs to the group and is not an outsider. She wants to
feel she means something to her husband. She needs to
feel adequate and worthwhile in her own right. Rightfully,
we are taught, "If your wife is short, bend down and
whisper to her." That is, man should not think of himself
as too superior to consult with his wife about his affairs. The
best way to care for a wife is to encourage her to function
to her fullest. Life is meant to be lived. The miser who
hoards it cheats only himself. Marriage can be likened to
a basket which is woven by interlacing husband and wife
with many ties. The size, shape, and beauty of this basket
varies, for its construction is a "do it yourself" project.
The durability and quality of the product will depend largely
upon the combination of ties involved and their skillful use.

So try to eliminate needless antagonisms. Get rid of the
chip on the shoulder. Stop listening to the relatives coaching
from the side-lines. Be just and fair. Sincerity and frank-
ness are to marriage, what honesty and integrity are to
business. Their presence insures success; their absence
leads to bankruptcy. Discuss your marital problems but
don't make this a daily diet of conversation. Develop areas
of agreement. Be a good sport. Smile more often. Develop
a sense of humor. Surrender your positions on non-essen-
tials. It isn't really important to have that last word. Permit

your spouse to develop ego satisfactions by developing and maintaining outside interests. Each of you must have an opportunity to feel important, wise, and intelligent. Keep improving yourself.

Husbands, if you adore her, adorn her. Show pleasure and satisfaction with her talents. Compliment her home-making ability. Make her relatives welcome in your home. Do not air your grievances in public. Be punctual at meals and appointments. Telephone her during the day and chat for a few minutes without giving specific instructions as to some chore you wish carried out. Say some of the things to her you used to say in your courting days. Date her! Court her! Don't take her for granted! Remember she may have come from one of your ribs, but not from your back-bone. And bear in mind the advice a Quaker once gave his son on his wedding day: "When thee went a-courting I told thee to keep thy eyes open; now that thou art married, I tell thee to keep them half shut."

Wives, don't make a big issue of his shortcomings. Don't criticize him in front of friends or family. When he starts telling a story, let him finish it even if you think you could do a better job. Don't gripe about entertaining his friends and relatives. Don't belittle his abilities as a husband or a provider. Christopher Morley's definition is right: "The plural of spouse is spice." Spice is seasoning, and adds taste to foods. Your married life needs spice. Don't spare it; spend it.

The Talmud reports the wise counsel given by a mother to a bride-to-be. "My daughter," she advised, "if you will respect your husband like a king, he will treat you like a queen. If you will serve him like a slave-girl, he will serve you like a slave. But if you will be too proud to serve him, he will treat you like a maid-servant. . . . If his friends come to his home, welcome them heartily. . . . Watch well your home and all your husband's possessions. He will be delighted with you and you will be the crown of his head."

In *Sotah* (3b), we find the necessary qualifications of a good wife: "A gentle temper, tact, modesty, and industry." A good wife is Heaven's best gift to a man; his angel of mercy, minister of finance; his gem of many virtues, his casket of jewels; her voice, his sweetest music; her smiles, his brightest day. She is the balm of his health, the essence of his life; her industry, his surest wealth; her economy, his safest steward; her prayers the ablest advocate of Heaven's blessing on his head. Is it any wonder that our holy writings state, "An unmarried man is not a man in the full sense," "A man's home is his wife," and finally, "The unmarried person lives without joy, without blessing, and without good."

Science has made great advances along certain lines. It is now possible to package the instant freshness of bread. The aroma of fresh coffee can be canned quickly to give delight when the container is opened. Luscious cakes can be placed in freezers to be defrosted days or weeks later. Grape juice, orange juice, peach nectar . . . all these fruit delights can be bottled to be used when desired at some later date. Canning, packaging and freezing have made it possible to capture and preserve culinary specialties and out of season delicacies. Now, if science could only discover some way to capture and preserve for future use, the warmth, love, understanding, tenderness, and joy of couples during their courtship period, to be used in measured quantities throughout the couple's lifetime, many marriages which now founder might be saved.

In Hebrew, there is no word for *marriage*. The word that is used for marriage is *kiddushin*, holiness. This is to signify that the relationship of man and woman in marriage is not a biological union alone, or an economic union, but rather a sacred oneness of man and woman united through the holiness of God. In the ideal married life there are not two partners but three. You, your beloved, and God. It is said that when a soul is sent down from Heaven it is a combined male and female soul. The male part enters the male child and the female part enters the female. If they are worthy, God causes them to reunite in marriage. This is true mating.

A marriage can yield lasting satisfactions. It can be rich in warmth and understanding, but it can never be the universal solution to all problems. Marriage does not basically change people. It can make a happy person happier, but it cannot be a unilateral solution to one's problems.

If you have a piece of wire too short to reach a desired point, you splice it. This is a simple procedure and one almost any amateur can do. But if you wish to make the splice firm and reasonably neat so the wire doesn't look as though it were wearing a fracture splint, you must take care and exercise good workmanship.

Marriage works pretty much the same way. Marriage can be successful if both partners never cease working for its success. It is like a garden. It requires attention every day to keep the weeds from ruining it. The happiest marriages are generally those where husband and wife are each eager to make the other happy. Marital happiness does not come packaged or ready made. It seems that people are willing to prepare diligently to become lawyers, plumbers, secretaries, but evidently not as candidates for a decent and lasting marriage. Marriage must be thought of as more than an adventure and more than a career. Marriage is a school of higher education for developing virtues to be used in the establishment of a good home.

CHAPTER SIXTEEN

May You Live to be 120

G ERIATRIC experts advise that men never grow old as long as they feel adequate, keep their sense of humor, and are actively interested in others. How old a person feels is largely determined by his evaluation of himself and by the attitudes of those around him. The real danger in reaching the sixties and seventies lies not in declining usefulness but in the defeatist attitudes that people have about aging. It follows that just sitting in a rocking-chair adds monotony as well as age to one's years. Older people should abhor being treated differently from others. They should resent being forced into retirement by unrealistic rules. Contrariwise, they should strive to remain active in the stream of life, to serve people, and to dive deeply into the water of community affairs. Old age to the unlearned and apathetic is famine; to the learned and curious it is harvest.

There are several categories of age, only one of which is easily measurable, and it is the least significant—chronological age. This is useful for birthday parties, legal and voting qualifications, getting a visa, a driving license, and very little else.

Biological aging is another category. This proceeds at different rates for different people. A man of fifty-five may have the body of a thirty-year old, the emotions of a forty year old, the knowledge of a sixty year old, and the learning capacity of a sixteen year old. Nature does not distribute energy equally. Some people are born old and tired, while others are going strong at seventy. This is what Oliver Wendell Holmes had in mind when he wrote, "To be seventy years young is sometimes far more cheerful and hopeful than to be forty years old." One man expressed it this way, "I'm not eighty years old at all. I am 4 times 20."

Who are the aged? What is middle age? In which age group do we classify ourselves? Today, we puzzle over such questions because the boundaries of age classifications have begun to break down. In 1930, author Walter B. Pitkin wrote a book called *Life Begins at 40*. Sales of this work climbed into the hundreds of thousands. It became an inspiration to an entire generation; a sort of renewal of the lease on life. To some extent, the title of the book is still a catch-phrase today.

But this is the late 20th century. This is the age of space travel, of miracle drugs, of speed. In the late 1960's, the phrase, "life begins at 40," is hopelessly out of date and offers little comfort to many people. Today, we would like to believe that life begins at 60. And the evidence is clear that tomorrow it will begin even later.

Science and medicine have added new years and offered new opportunities to everyone's life. Men and women have banished many of the old fears and old burdens that plagued their grandfathers almost a century ago. Studies made in leading universities indicate that "maximum satisfaction and gratification in life" come at about age 50. The high point of maturity actually is reached around 50, according to other studies made at the University of Minnesota. "Older workers' output not only rivals that of younger people in quantity, but also in quality, and they have a steadier production rate. Workers 65 and over generally average as high as any other group," states the Bureau of Labor Statistics. These studies seem to indicate that 50 is the mid-point in life, when as many productive adult years lie ahead as lie behind. But they are vastly different years. The period of establishment lies in the years up to the age of 50. The time to capitalize on the experience, skills, and knowledge stockpiled earlier lies in the years after the age of 50.

Only thirty years ago, a man of 50 traveled the slow road to decline. He anticipated poor health, shrinking income, and continuing responsibilities. He was scorned as "too old!" and barred from progress with the sentence, "You can't teach an old dog new tricks." Today, you may find men of sixty taking swimming lessons; women of sixty attending adult classes; people of fifty directing and participating in civic and charitable organizations. Lincoln wrote of himself as old at 48, two years before he was elected president. After that date, he never mentioned his age; he was too busy running the country.

Are you 50? If you are, here is what is in store for you. You can look ahead to long life, better health, and more job opportunities. Industry and the nation demand men of experience as well as young men's brawn. A new value has been placed on experience and wisdom, which only older people have. A 34-year old surgeon was asked what special qualities were required for success in his profession. "The first qualification is 25 years of experience," he replied. One reason for this new type of thinking is that the old notion of intelligence declining with age has been debunked. Studies show that intelligence reaches a peak at 40 and that the capacity to learn continues for years.

Life, today, begins at 50; begins for those who have the courage to accept the challenge; who continue to learn and do; who recognize that in middle age one can be active and articulate in social and political affairs; who refuse to write themselves off. Tools shaped by 50 years of living, fashion the new life desired.

Each decade of a person's life has different goals, which are determined chiefly by the energy demanded. In the life pattern, breadth of interest gradually changes to depth of interest. Middle age constitutes the picture that can be painted with oils accumulated during the earlier decades.

Age need not be a period of life in which a man loses his hair, teeth, initiative, illusions and what little patience he once had. Perhaps one cannot help being old, but one can resist being aged A man was once advised by his friend, "In the central place of your heart there is a wireless station. So long as it receives messages of beauty, strength, courage, joy, and understanding from fellow-men, you are young." Old age can be avoided by talking about new thoughts and by throwing off old habits. Having a purpose in life distinguishes those persons who grow old from those who get old. Moses was eighty when he came before Pharoah. Rabbi Akiba began studying at forty and was highly active in his career when he was well past one hundred.

To grow old gracefully is to make a necklace of a happy useful life on which each bead is a year of purposeful living. When a man has come to the point at which he no longer believes that there is anything worth seeing, he is old. He certainly is aged when he does more and more for the last time, and less and less for the first time.

The key word to youth is enthusiasm. In order to maintain a youthful spirit in middle age, one must feel there are many wonders still to be seen, many books still to be read, many friends still to be made, many organizations still to be helped and many goals still to be achieved. A recent analysis of achievement of 400 famous men throughout history encouraged many who thought they were growing old. The study revealed that more than one-third in this group achieved their greatest accomplishments after they

passed the age of sixty. A surprising 23% scored their
greatest success in life after the age of seventy.

Real happiness in the golden years can come only with
the creation of proper attitudes. A wholesome philosophy
of life can provide inner resources needed to meet changing
life situations. The tools of later life are established during
youth. If it is sensible for the child to make an effort to
learn how to be an adult, then it is essential for the adult
to learn how to be aged. The truth is you really don't
grow old. When you cease to grow, you *are* old.

To this we might add:

"Lord, Thou knowest that we are growing older. Keep
us from becoming talkative and possessed with the
idea that we must express ourselves on every subject.
Release us from the craving to straighten out everyone's affairs. Seal our lips when we are inclined to
tell of aches and pains. They are increasing with the
years and our love to speak of them grows sweeter as
time goes by. Teach us the glorious lesson that occasionally we may be wrong. Make us thoughtful but not
nosy—helpful but not bossy. With our vast store of
wisdom and experience, give us opportunities to serve
others. Thou knowest Lord that we do not wish to be
alone, that we wish to feel adequate and useful. Motivate us then to travel, visit, plan, work, read, and live
every day of the years with which You have blessed
us. AMEN!"

CHAPTER SEVENTEEN

Freud, Adler, and Our Rebbes

A LFRED ADLER, one of Freud's disciples, stated that happiness depended on satisfactory conditions in three areas of life, *society, sustenance,* and *sex.* It was his clinical opinion that the neurotic could be diagnosed from his failures in these three areas. He felt that an individual must be social-minded, must be aware of the people around him, must want to mix and be part of a growing community. The person who withdrew from human relations was the one who was on his way to mental failure.

In *Understanding Human Nature,* Adler writes, "We may now understand that any rules that serve to secure the existence of mankind, such as legal codes, education, must be governed by the concept of the community and be appropriate to it. . . . We can judge a character as bad or good only from the standpoint of society. The criteria by which we can measure an individual are determined by his value to mankind in general. We compare an individual with the ideal picture of a fellowman, a man who overcomes the tasks and difficulties which lie before him, in a way which is useful to society in general, a man who has developed his social feeling to a high degree. He is one who plays the game of life according to the laws of society. In the course of our demonstrations it will become increasingly evident that no adequate man can grow up without cultivating a deep sense of fellowship in humanity and practicing the art of being a human being."

Our own sacred writings are full of good, practical psychiatric advice along the same lines. What psychiatrists and psychologists are now discovering has been uttered hundreds, if not thousands of years ago.

Man was not intended to live alone but as a member of society, is advice that can be read almost anywhere in our writings. Ample illustrations are offered by our rabbis as to just what this rule entails. "A person is a unit in the body of humanity," they claim, "and this fact creates many duties for him with respect to his relationship with his fellow-men. His life is not his own to do with as he pleases. His conduct affects his neighbors as their conduct affects him." It is like a company of men on board a ship. One of them took a drill and began to bore a hole under him. The other passengers were worried. One said to him, "What are you doing?"

He replied, "What has that to do with you? Am I not making the hole under my seat?"

"Yes," they retorted, "but the water will enter and drown us all."

"An isolated life is not worth living," advised Choni the Circle-drawer, the Rip Van Winkle of the Talmud. Since the life of man has grown more complex, man's requirements are so many that he must realize how much of his comfort he owes to the toil of others. In *Ecclesiastes* (iv,9) the advice is given, "Two are better than one." "Separate not yourself from the community," (*Aboth* ii, 5) was the advice of Hillel. Cooperation and mutual assistance are essential factors in life, as a proverb tells us, "If you will lift the load I will lift it too; but if you will not lift it, I will not."

A Talmudic proverb likewise counselled, "If you have entered a city conform to its laws"; and the rabbis turned to the Bible for corroboration in a curious manner: "A man should never depart from established practice; behold, when Moses ascended above he did not eat (*Exod.* xxxiv, 28), and when the ministering angels descended to earth they partook of food (*Gen.* xviii,8)."

The ethical wills of some of the greatest rabbis of blessed memory contain a wealth of good advice as to how an individual can be social-minded. In 1544, Rabbi Eleazar the Great published a work which he called *Paths of Life.* Part of it might be called an ethical will directed to his son. The advice might very well be a listing prepared by a psychologist.

He writes, among many other items, the following:

"My Son!
Take heed to hold constant intercourse with the wise. Rely not on thine own opinion.

Be zealous in visiting the sick, for sympathy lightens pain.
Bear thy part regularly in the burial of the dead, delivering them into the hand of their Maker.
Comfort the mourners, and speak to their heart.
Join in bringing the bride to the canopy, help to gladden the bridegroom.
Show honor to the poor, and draw out thy soul unto him.
Crush not the poor with harsh words.
Stop not thine ears at the cry of the poor, for he who is deaf to the appeal of others, when he crieth shall himself obtain no answer.

Make not thyself too much feared in thine home.
Love the wise and attach thyself to them.
Walk not alone, judge not alone, testify not alone, nor be witness and judge at the same time."

These are some basic rules which we would do well to follow. We ought to remember that knowledge without common sense is folly; without method it is waste; without kindness it is fanaticism; without religion it is death. But with common sense, it is wisdom; with method it is power; with character it is beneficence; with *religion,* it is *virtue, life,* and *peace.*

The question usually asked is, "Why was there no need for psychotherapists years ago?" In truth, there was such a need, and this type of service was provided for by the *rebbe.* He listened. He advised. He consoled. He was the therapist because there was great rapport between the Jew and his *rebbe.* He wasn't called a psychologist, psychoanalyst, or psychiatrist but he had a bit of all three in his makeup.

With the help of the *rebbe,* the Jew was made to understand the reasons for his living. The *rebbe* became the camera lens through which the Jew saw life. He taught that life was not a corridor with only a single door opening at the farthest end. He helped him fashion new insights, helped him form an estimate of himself, helped him set up new values in life.

And above all, Judaism, with its emphasis on group worship, on community solidarity, on man's responsibility for his brothers, provided and still provides its adherents with a natural framework for healthy psychological development.

CHAPTER EIGHTEEN

Vitamins for Personality

PERSONALITY is molded in early years. A child who has had an improper diet during his early youth carries the marks throughout his life, in physiological deficiencies of bone structure or in lack of muscular strength. In the same manner, the personality that is starved or mistreated during the early years will bear throughout life the marks of early deprivation. Personality does not spring up overnight. It is the outcome of situations met, challenges accepted, duties done; the sum of many days well used.

The early years are significant because it is at this time that the basic personality structure is being formed and its capacity for growing and functioning is being fashioned. The best heritage a child can have is to be born into a home where there is normal family life with parents who withhold their own disappointments from the ears and eyes of the children. A child who runs into a hot radiator will carry a physical scar; the child who is exposed to the bitterness of fighting parents will carry a scar for the rest of his life. Happy laughter and friendly voices in the home are the best health tonics a child can have.

What are the vitamins for good personality development? A list of basic needs for proper personality development includes the following:

Need for Self-Respect

Glass blowers will never produce anything as fragile as the human ego. There can be no constructive living from a person who lacks self-respect. Self-respect is the cement of mental health. All of us need to think well of ourselves. We need others to think well of us. It is wrong to shame children. It is wrong to belittle their abilities and bury their talents. Statements such as

"Aren't you ashamed of yourself?"
"Look at that ugly face of yours!"
"Why did God punish me with a child like you?"
"Shut up! Who cares what you think!"
"How can one person be so stupid?"

become drills in self-depreciation. It would be far more advantageous to emphasize a child's strengths. The "pat-on-the-back" in many instances brings positive results.

Need for Freedom

We live in a democracy where there is great freedom. Adults have sacrificed their lives so that freedom could be preserved. Wars have been fought for this principle. God Himself freed the Jews from the Egyptian yoke.

Children, too, need a certain amount of freedom if they are to mature into thinking, responsible adults. The story is told about a boy who was asked by a visitor, "Son, what is your name?"

"Daniel don't," replied the child.

Children need physical and psychological freedom. They learn through their own errors. They need a chance to let off steam after the school day.

Need for Love and Affection

Tender loving care (TLC) has long been a favorite prescription of psychiatrists, psychologists and guidance counselors. All of us need love and affection in our lives. We are alive today only because someone cared enough to keep us alive when we were infants. Every child needs adults in his life who love him, and for whom he has genuine, spontaneous affection. A parent need not talk about love. He should rather spell it out with actions.

Need to Belong

Most of us are joiners. We belong to a group, a club, a family, a team, a house of worship. We feel strength in belonging and being accepted. Little children feel important when they do what adults are doing. If mother is baking a cake, four-year-old Rivka will want to make one too. If father is building a cabinet, little Sammy will be hammering boards together. In this way he feels he belongs. This is how a child attempts to identify with a parent.

Need to Be Needed

Writers have often discussed the fact that a child should have a sense of security, a sense of adequacy. The child should feel he has a place in the family group. He can only feel this way if he carries his share of responsibility. The child who does not contribute to the family cannot be made to feel secure or adequate. He is a parasite and feels he is of little value.

There is no sure way to guarantee that your child will grow up to be the kind of person you would like him to be. The best way is for *you* to be the kind of person you would like him to be. In addition, you must provide him with a healthy and a happy home. Let it be a religious home where God is a frequent visitor; let it be filled with love; enforce your "do's and don't's"; relieve monotony; make all members contributing members of the household; emphasize genuine values; share with others; give all a chance to grow up. What the world needs most today is happy homes. Not rich homes. Not frustrated homes. Not empty homes, but homes where the emphasis lies not on what we've done, but on the work we've just begun. The home, not the individual, is the first unit of society. Every person enters the world in a social circle of at least three. The family came first in history. Government started there. Discipline began there and still begins there. A strong home gives strength and stability to any society.

The family circle is the child's first and most important school, and parents are the world's most influential teachers. What happens to a child later in life, from the crime he commits to the emotional illness to which he falls heir, can be traced directly or indirectly to those indelible years when he was in the hands of his parents.

The Jewish home is a sphere where love rules but where proper discipline is maintained. It takes more than beautiful walls and comfortable furniture to make a home. To grow up in a home where God is known, loved, honored and recognized daily in consistent living means more than wealth or fame. A happy home is more than a roof over your child's head—it's a foundation under his feet.

CHAPTER NINETEEN

Words Too Are Deadly

THE Midrash tells the story of the rabbi who disguised himself as an itinerant vendor of herbs and spices, and going into the market place, proclaimed his wares, crying, *"sam chaim, sam chaim!* The spice of life! The elixir of life! Who wishes to buy the secret of eternal life?" Attracted by his cry, a large crowd gathered around him asking for the secret. The noise reached Rabbi Yannai who was studying a difficult passage of the Torah. He opened his window and called to the vendor, "Tell me the secret!"

The man took from his sack the Book of Psalms and opening it to Psalm 34 said: "Here is my merchandise: 'Who wishes to live, guard thy tongue from evil and thy lips from speaking deceit; do good, seek peace.' This is the secret."

Yannai thanked him for the interpretation and quoted the verse from Proverbs: "Whoso guardeth his mouth and his tongue keeps his soul from trouble."

Years ago, when the Jewish theatre was at its best, Jacob Gordon wrote and produced a play called, *"Gott, Mensch, and Taivel"*—God, Man, and Devil. In the play, the devil was not represented with a horn and a tail, carrying a pitchfork. On the contrary, the author indicated that the *taivel* could be anyone. The next-door neighbor might even qualify, if the neighbor was a gossip, a slanderer, a tale-bearer.

Playwright Gordon was not the first to speak out against the gossip. Our rabbis, over and over again, have expressed

117

their deep contempt and thorough displeasure for this vicious, weak-minded individual. "God loves not tale-bearers.
. . . The tale-bearer is a cannibal," advises Ibn Ezra in
Shirat Yisrael. "A gossip is like an infidel," writes Jose
b. Zimra. In *Sanhedrin* we read that four types of people
do not receive the presence of the *Shechinah*: scorners, liars,
flatterers, and slanderers. In other words, if abstention
from evil speech is *sam chaim,* addiction to it is *sam mavet,*
elixir of death. Our rabbis wrote, "All animals will one
day remonstrate with the serpent and say, 'The lion treads
upon his prey and devours it. The wolf tears and eats it,
but you, what profit have you in biting?" The serpent will
reply, 'I am no worse than the slanderer who destroys
without reason or benefit.' "

A great deal of the trouble in the world is created by
things people say and write. Words of hate, envy, jealousy,
resentment cause people to lash back. The world is too
dangerous for anything but the truth, and too small for
anything but brotherhood.

Who is a gossip? A gossip is usually an inadequate,
frustrated, unhappy, incompetent soul whose greatest joy
is fishing in dirty waters. He is the neurotic personality
who does not feel equal to the demands of life because he
is bothered by a deep-seated inferiority complex. He attempts to compensate for his sense of inadequacy, seeking
to rise by depreciating others through the insidious exercise
of his vicious tongue. Slandering others serves to boost his
sagging ego. Alfred Adler called this technique the Deroga-
tory Critique—a technique used by one who thinks it is
easier to besmirch and defile another than it is to lift oneself up by meritorious achievement.

The gossip is a social vulture, a producer of evil who
may wear the mask of the saint, the reformer, the perfect
friend, the ultimate authority. In reality, he is Public

Enemy No. 1 and can be recognized by his unbridled contempt for others, by his complete lack of honesty and sincerity. Every social circle has a tale-bearer, who lives like a soldier's dog on the bits and scraps he picks up in the barracks. Since the dog wags no man's tail but his own, he, at least, is honorable.

The gossip and tale-bearer set on fire all the houses they enter. They destroy homes, wreck marriages, and dissolve friendships. In the Bible, an evil tongue is compared to an arrow rather than to a sword. The reason is that a sword can wound only one who is near and actually feels its point; but an arrow flies abroad and wounds from afar. Slander, too, has no limit. It goes afar and its effect extends far beyond the place whence it emanates.

The gossip can be compared to a stream that seeks its own level and eventually finds it in the sewer. There is no greater nuisance than the gossip, because his underhanded attacks deface the landscape of life like a swarm of locusts. He is a sea of mud disfiguring and dirtying everything he touches. Nothing is more dangerous than his kind of vagrant aggression, which originates from self-hate, inadequacy, insecurity, and blind jealousy. It was with keen wisdom that Jeremy Taylor wrote, "Every man has in his own life sins enough, in his own mind trouble enough, so that curiosity after the affairs of others cannot be without envy and an evil mind."

The great Maimonides, Rabbi Moshe ben Maimon, who lived some 800 years ago, wrote, "The sin of the man with the evil tongue is worse than the murderer, since the slanderer destroys a man's reputation which is more precious than life. He kills with his tongue three victims: himself, the man listening to his slander, and the innocent victim."

Jacob Gordon was right. The *taivel* need not wear horns nor have a tail. He might very well be your next-door neighbor, or one of your acquaintances. Simply explained, it is dangerous to be in the company of a gossip, because today he brings to you a story about a third party. Tomorrow, he might very well reverse the procedure. A slanderer must be treated like a leper. Isolate him from society because his tongue is contagious. He must be taught that leprosy of the mind is as fatal as leprosy of the body, that it is impossible to sling mud with clean hands. It might be said that if you have a gossip for a friend, you don't need any enemies.

CHAPTER TWENTY

Do We Like What We See?

FOR years now, there has been a campaign to raise children in an atmosphere free from criticism, repression, and guilt. We have been told repeatedly that a permissive environment is necessary if a child's personality is to develop freely. The poor confused parent has been exposed to lectures, pamphlets, magazine articles, books—all proclaiming the virtue of permissiveness. It has been indicated that in this way a child's real talents will emerge and he will be able to express himself freely and grow to the limit of his native endowment.

Isn't it high time for parents and teachers alike to stand back and examine the progress made, to evaluate results, take inventory? What do we see? As we look at the uninhibited child, can we in all honesty say we approve of him? Is he disciplined? Does he understand his place in the family and at school? Is he a contributing member of some group? Does he know how to share? Does he fully understand and accept the word, "NO?"

If it is true that the child who grows up under a rigid rule will, as an adult, be inhibited and unable to live a full life, it is equally true that the child who has his own way, will grow up to be a selfish egocentric, unable to mix in society, knowing no consideration for others. While it is true that children need love and encouragement, it is equally true that they need a firm rein, and must experience hard lessons. If they do not learn when they are young, they will suffer bitterly when they are older. Parents who do not provide the difficult task as well as the loving guidance, do their children no real favor. They simply delegate to others the painful task of training children for life's realities.

Parents and teachers alike face a real challenge today. This is not a challenge to return to the "3 R's" of our fathers, but to develop human beings who are able to live with themselves and their neighbors. This precludes a situation in which children get everything at little or no cost to themselves. If a child is not taught self-control in the home, the grown-up world will take care of him later on, perhaps cruelly, and when it is too late.

We must cease being soft and indulgent with our children, because this results in failure to inculcate perseverance, industry, and conscientiousness. We must remind our children of the commandment, "Honor thy father and thy mother." We must point out that this commandment was written on the same tablet on which our duties towards God were engraven, because the honor due to these representatives of God equals that which we owe Him.

Let us be more concerned with our children's future effectiveness in life and less concerned with their present happiness. Children have to learn that there is more to life than play, but it does take a lot of work on the part of parents to convince them. An old railroader once said, "A switch has put many a delinquent on the right track." This is far better than sending junior to his room, because the chances are that in his room he has his own radio, phonograph, and television set.

We must be honest with children about the facts of life, of birth, and of death. We must help them to be honest about their feelings, their goals, their interests, their curiosities, and their worries. We must help them accept themselves as they are, individuals with limitations of talent and ability. We must instill self-confidence and the proper attitude toward work and duty. If criticism must be given, we should at least give it in the same proportion as praise.

Being a parent is a full-time job. If we parents took more time and interest in our children, we would not have nearly as much delinquency as there now is all over the country. Parental delinquency often times leads to juvenile delinquency. It takes a great deal of patience to bring up children properly. It takes love and understanding. Parents should discuss their children's problems with them and help them in their youthful crises. Even at an early age, children are much wiser than we think.

Some years ago, a definition of a good parent was prepared. How many of the following characteristics apply to you?

Good Parents Are

1. Parents who try to understand their children and find the time to cultivate their friendship and love.
2. Parents of integrity who face facts and live by the truth.
3. Parents who live within their means and give their children examples of thrift, security, and stability.
4. Parents who are industrious and teach their children that most of life's good things come only from hard work.
5. Parents who have worthwhile goals in life and seek to have their children join them in their attainments.
6. Parents who have common sense, a capacity for friendship, and a sense of humor.
7. Parents who live in harmony with each other, and do not quarrel in the presence of their children.
8. Parents who have ideals and a more compelling urge to serve, than be served.

9 Parents whose decisions are controlled, not by what their children desire, but by what they need.

10. Parents who are unswervingly loyal to their children but who can express righteous indignation and chastise them when necessary. The old proverb, "Spare the rod and spoil the child" is as valid today as it ever was.

Socrates must have dipped into the writings of the sages when he proclaimed, "If I could get to the highest place in Athens, I would lift my voice and say, 'What mean ye, fellow citizens, that ye turn every stone to scrape wealth together, and take so little care of your children, to whom ye must one day relinquish all!'"

If you wish to be a more effective parent—a good parent from "A" to "Z"—the following pattern is suggested:

A *Accomplishments*:
Show sincere interest in the accomplishments of your children.

B *Books*:
Books should be introduced into a child's life right along with toys, dolls, and bike.

C *Conscience*:
When children are young they need to be provided with a conscience just as they need to be provided with food and shelter.

D *Develop a Sense of Humor*:
Laugh at yourself once in a while. It makes you human in the eyes of your children.

E *Environment*:
A child cannot be brought up under a glass jar. His unhappy experiences will not hurt him if he is surrounded by warmth and the feeling of being loved.

F *Family Responsibilities:*
Give a child a chore, a household task, so that he can feel he is a contributing member of the family.

G *Good Music:*
Childhood is the time when a parent can best inculcate a taste for good music.

H *Habits:*
Adult behavior and thinking is developed from habits learned as children. Integrity, persistence, respectfulness and friendliness are learned early in life.

I *Incentives:*
Reward children for good work done, but do not bribe them for doing it.

J *Jealousy:*
Watch for signs of jealousy between sisters and brothers. A frank open discussion will help all of the family.

K *Knowledge:*
The child becomes the kind of person he is through knowledge. He learns from his experiences.

L *Love:*
The child needs love as much as he needs food, if he is to develop properly. Without love in his early years, he will be unable to give love to others.

M *Manners:*
Manners represent learned behavior. Parents must practice good manners at home.

N *"No!":*
The use of the parental "NO" is a basic positive factor in a child's development. However, it should not be abused and overdone.

O *Open House:*
Make your home a happy home; one so attractive that your child will bring his friends there.

P   Praise:

Give him a "pat on the back" when necessary, or better yet, when deserved. Select for praise specific instances of good conduct in which the child has done with effort what is considered meritorious.

Q   Question:

Question your own attitude from time to time. Take inventory of how you handle your children. As the rabbis say, "With one hand push away and the other bring nearer to you."

R   Respect-Responsibiility:

Two "R's" that should be taught along with Reading, 'Riting, and 'Rithmetic are *respect* and *responsibility*.

S   Strengths:

Build on a child's strengths rather than on his weaknesses. The more successes he achieves in his youth, the greater will his chances be for success as an adult.

T   Togetherness:

Do things together. Plan a family gathering, a picnic in the country, or a family attendance at a concert.

U   Understanding:

This is a sort of radar system between you and your family that will signal feelings and attitudes.

V   Values:

Teach moral and ethical values by example. The young child gets his values and his basic attitudes toward people and life at home. If the values of the home and the school are consistent, he has an easy time of it.

W   Worship:

Go to *shul* together. Why should mother, dad, and children go to three separate synagogues?

X   'Xamine:

Yes, as mother would say, 'xamine your conduct and your thoughts.

Y *Yenem:*

Avoid comparisons between your children and other children. They never or seldom ever spur your child to greater endeavors.

Z *Zest:*

If all the other letters of the alphabet are present in your daily conduct, your children and you will have the *zest* to do and to live.

CHAPTER TWENTY-ONE

How to Raise a Delinquent

OUR children suffer today not from physical and economic poverty, but rather from emotional and spiritual bankruptcy. Children have everything money can buy. They are refused nothing, that is, except discipline and guidance. Today's youngsters have their own rooms, completely equipped playrooms in the finished basement, adequate allowances. Seldom is a wish of theirs denied.

When it comes to a matter of discipline, however, the parent is more than negligent. He lacks the desire or the willingness to take the time to teach his children. If parents won't discipline a child, the world, at some later date, will. Unfortunately when this occurs it comes with devastating consequences. The individual is not prepared for what happens. He had been permitted to believe that discipline was for his neighbors, not himself.

Experts now agree that children need parents who can be firm; who can and do use the word, "NO!" A youngster asks only to be taught the boundaries of acceptable behavior. Discipline, fairly and consistently invoked, breeds pride and respect. Children want to be disciplined.

Juvenile delinquency is increasing. There has never been a moment in our history when adults have been more shocked than they are today by the unprecedented wave of bad behavior among children. There are teenage muggings, senseless killings, gang warfare, destruction of private and public property and a rise of venereal disease in the

128

15 to 19 year age group. The roots of juvenile delinquency apparently run very deep.

The problem of juvenile delinquency has been widely discussed in the press, but little reference has been made to adult delinquency, that is, the inability of parents to discharge their full parental obligation in the upbringing of their sons and daughters. Delinquency is a measure of adult neglect of children, for children were alright when we got them.

Juvenile delinquency results when parents try to train children without starting at the bottom. A parent must set a boundary within which his child may act. He must once again return the word "NO!" to the family vocabulary. Adults understand that freedom of speech doesn't allow one individual to slander another. They understand that right of private property doesn't give one the right to drive down a one-way street the wrong way. There are laws which help us understand that when we invade the rights of other people, we will be punished.

Dr. Marjorie Rittwagen, the staff psychiatrist of New York City's Children's Court, considers that there are four main causes of delinquency:

1. Neglectful, disturbed parents;
2. Crowded neighborhoods with shifting populations;
3. Inadequate schools;
4. Absence of any beliefs and values among children.

While it is true that religious institutions play a great part in the moral guidance of the young, the onus falls upon the parent at home. Greater and more responsible supervision by parents will finally be the cure for juvenile delinquency.

The police department of one of our municipal governments listed the causes for delinquency in language most parents can understand and appreciate. They are:

1. Begin with infancy to give the child everything he wants. In this way he will grow up to believe that the world owes him a living.

2. When he picks up bad words, laugh at him. This will make him think he is cute. It will also encourage him to pick up "cuter" phrases that will blow up the top of your head later.

3. Never give him any religious training. Wait until he is twenty-one and then let him "decide for himself."

4. Avoid use of the word "wrong." It may develop a guilt complex. This will condition him to believe later, when he is arrested for stealing a car, that society is against him and he is being persecuted.

5. Pick up everything he leaves lying around—books, shoes, clothes and newspapers. Do everything for him so that he will be experienced in throwing all responsibility on others.

6. Let him read any printed matter he can get his hands on. Be careful that the silverware and drinking glasses are sterilized, but let his mind feast on garbage.

7. Quarrel frequently in the presence of your children. In this way they will not be shocked when the home is broken up later.

8. Give a child all the spending money he wants. Never let him earn his own. Why should he have things as tough as you had them?

9. Satisfy his every craving for food, drink and comfort. See that every sensual desire is gratified. Denial may lead to harmful frustration.

10. Take his part against neighbor and teacher. They are all prejudiced against your child.

A parent cannot live life for his child, but he can equip him with the courage, the strength, the discipline, the morality, the duty to meet life's challenges, to accept them, and to overcome them. It is in the home and within the family circle that the habits of life are cultivated and the basic attitudes towards society are shaped and developed. Parents are not obligated to give their children a secure future, but they are obligated to give them a secure foundation on which to build their future. If you fashion a crutch for someone, he may use it all his life. If you show him how to walk, crippled as he may be, he will learn to overcome his handicap. Many parents have forever crippled their children by an oversupply of crutches.

The rabbis taught that he who begets the child is not called father—only he who trains and raises up the child. We are taught, "My son, keep the commandment of thy father and forsake not the law of thy mother. When thou walkest it shall lead thee; when thou sleepest it shall watch over thee; and when thou wakest it shall talk with thee." Perhaps it is well for parents to keep in mind that no greater gift can be given a child than the ability and know-how to serve the Almighty. Along the way, the child will also learn how to respect his parents.

CHAPTER TWENTY-TWO

You Can Kill With Kindness

A MAKER of violins searched all his life for wood that would be best suited for making instruments which produced a certain beautiful, haunting resonance. He found what he was looking for in the wood gathered from the timberline of a great mountain range, the last stand of trees growing 12,000 feet above sea level. Up there, where the winds blew so fiercely and steadily that the bark had no chance to form, where the branches all pointed one way, and where a tree to live had to remain bowed down all through its life, grew the world's most resonant wood. It survived because it had learned to overcome the difficulties and dangers of its environment.

Perhaps a lesson in child rearing can be learned from this story. Today, parents are eager to protect their children from failure and frustration. They do all but live their children's lives, and in some cases, perhaps, do that as well. They select schools, courses, teachers, friends; suggest hobbies; prescribe books to be read; and very often do research reports. "I will give my child everything I didn't have," is the motto emblazoned on the family crest.

Children cannot be brought up in this hot-house protective atmosphere. It might do for plants and flowers but it is harmful to children. The psychologist advises, "The normal, healthy child stretches out its arms to life. He reaches out toward the bad and the good, toward the fire, the water, the poison. He has to learn what is good and what is bad. But in the teaching, the child is not to be made timid. A child should be taught not mere fear of fire, but the proper use of it; not mere fear of water, but how to swim." After all, building children is better than mending men.

Parents cannot afford to overindulge their children. In fact, overindulgence is the ultimate insult, for when you spoil a child, you are in reality saying to the child, "You just aren't capable of being social, civilized and considerate, so I can't expect it of you." This type of treatment will cause your child to be apprehensive, tense, and insecure. The Bratzlaver Rebbe advised, "Children will be healthy and well-bred, if parents do not play with them overmuch and do not indulge them too generously."

In Judaism, the importance of the parent-child relationship is stressed. Over and over again our sages emphasize the responsibility of the parent. The Hebrew word for parents is *horim* and it comes from the same root as *moreh*, teacher. The parent is the most effective teacher that the child will ever have. It is from the parent that the child will learn how to face life's problems.

Every child should be a contributing member of a household and should be a taxpayer as well. He can make payment with money, services, or both. The amount he contributes should be determined by his age and capability. No free loaders should be tolerated. Getting without giving is poor preparation for life.

A child needs training in the skill of exercising his own judgment. He can do this only if opportunities are presented to him to make decisions. He should be motivated to think for himself, and should be afforded opportunities for self-direction. He should have his share of responsibilities and should be expected to live up to them. Children, as far as possible, should have an environment in which they feel happy, not thwarted. They should have instruction to the degree that their abilities warrant.

Parents should encourage their children to think for themselves and should allow young people to take upon themselves a reasonable amount of responsibility for home welfare. They should, by words and actions, make it clear that they, as parents, are aware of their children's developing maturity. Young children have unlimited curiosity. Whether or not their curiosity leads to worthwhile interests depends very largely on the behavior of the adults about them.

In a well-adjusted family, parents don't permit a parasitic situation to develop. On the contrary, children are encouraged to take expanding responsibilities. In this way parents don't live for children, but rather with them.

A parent is duty bound to devote a certain amount of time to the rearing of children. He has to help his child develop into a person, who though studious, is sociable; though self-confident, is modest; though independent, is not eccentric. A child's character is built by the bricks of habit he piles up each day. Each brick may seem a little thing, but before very long, he may have shaped the house in which he will live.

The objectives of modern education may be stated as the "7 R's": Reading, 'Riting, 'Rithmetic, Reasoning, Responsibility, Resourcefulness and Realization of the importance of achieving worthy goals and purposes. These objectives represent the true aim of education.

The phonograph record gives back what it has received and recorded. If good music is played to it in its rubber disc stage, good music will be given back at the proper time. If however, the rubber disc was exposed to uncouth, vulgar discord, these are the sounds it will some day give back. This is the parable of human life. What a child absorbs in his youth he reflects in his maturity. What he receives during his plastic years, he later returns to the world.

What presents can we parents give our children? We can give them first and before everything else the memory of a happy home. We can create for them, day by day, and hour by hour, an atmosphere of love, tenderness, and unselfishness. We can give them tasks, give them training, give them the inspiration of devoted lives. We need not worry so much about accumulating money so that we can leave them a fortune. If we must leave a fortune, let it be a fortune of memories, inspiration, example, and hopes, so that they may be rich in heart, brain, soul, and service to the community.

A rabbi made a habit of presenting to his grown children a pair of scales. The children wondered why their father had selected scales as a sign of maturity. The rabbi exclaimed: "A pair of scales is one of the most important things in life. If you tend to be too gay and carefree, see to it that you balance the scales with more serious aspects in life."

A wonderful story sermon indeed. The family circle is the child's first and most important school, and parents are the world's most influential teachers.

CHAPTER TWENTY-THREE

Are Our Children Facing a Moral Breakdown?

THE vast majority of our young folks are making a genuine, constructive effort to live right, act right, and perform useful roles in home and community life; and to mold themselves into adults capable of effectively bearing responsibility as citizens and assuming leadership in the future. No one can deny that from this group will come our surgeons, statesmen, rabbis, teachers, and business executives. This group will produce men of vision, leadership, and skill; men who will help fashion a new and better world.

We realize, of course, that among the minority, there are serious problems to be dealt with, including among other things, an increase in delinquency. The statistics in this area are alarming. There is cause to be fearful of where the youth of today is heading, what it will do with its great material abundance and unlimited opportunity for good or evil.

The moral breakdown among our youth is so alarming that F.B.I. Director J. Edgar Hoover has called it a crisis which threatens the very future of our people. The White House Conference on Children and Youth uncovered some alarming facts. Juvenile delinquency is increasing five times faster than the child population of juvenile age; teenagers bear 40% of all the illegitimate children in the United States; juveniles under 18 represented 12% of all persons arrested, and accounted for 64.1% of auto thefts, 49.9% of burglaries, 48.5% of larceny cases, and 22% of robbery charges.

What has happened to our children? Where has society failed them? Where have they failed themselves?

Can it be that with our feverish preoccupation with secular studies, our emphasis on mathematics and science, medicine and law, on placing a man in orbit, we run the risk of spawning a race of human automatons, human robots, human *golems?*

Can it be that we have placed too much stock in material success for its own sake, and that our children today, physically fit though they may be, morally reflect the worship of success to the exclusion of other values an earlier generation was taught to venerate?

Can it be that in our relentless emphasis on the individual (emphasized by society in the form of state scholarships, medals, honor certificates, dean's lists), our children have only inadequately learned the solemn obligations of the individual to his parents, his elders, his siblings, his community, and his religion?

Can it be that our children have grown up in too much of an atmosphere of ridicule and disdain for the simple virtues of home and family? Have they forgotten how to plan and dream? Are they so preoccupied with the present that they are blinded to the vision of tomorrow? Is it possible that our children are so concerned with satisfying immediate desires that they do not conceive of higher goals, worthy of great dedication? Have our children lost all interest in the values of yesterday—in truth, in concern for others, in living a moral life?

The over-all problem facing our youth is materialistic atheism. A de-spiritualizing process has taken place. Our children have been indoctrinated with a false outlook on life. They neglect to show gratitude for the heritage of the past, and for the sacrifices of their parents.

This then is the problem. What is the solution?

As adults, we have the responsibility of setting good examples. Too few of us can say, "My son, give me thy heart. And let thine eyes observe my ways." We need to improve the moral climate in which the youth of today is accumulating ideas, ideals, and knowledge upon which to conduct an adult life. It is only right for them to look to the adult for the moral bricks with which to build the future.

The principal responsibility that rests upon parents is to educate children to become cultured members of the human race; to forge them into secure links in the chain of continuity, so that moral principles bequeathed by the preceding generations can be transmitted to the generations to follow.

Yet there are adults who are corrupting young lives, corrupting them with acts of commission and omission. An alarming percentage of children are maturing without an adequate sense of right and wrong. There seems to be a lack of parental authority. Many adults do not have values for themselves and are unable to set values for their children.

We must once again relearn that the family is the basis of society; that the father is the head of the house and that mother's primary obligation is to her home, and not to some social, charitable, or business organization.

"And they shall make Me a sanctuary; and I will dwell in the midst of them" (*Exod.* xxv,8), may very well refer to the Jewish home—the home in which dwells a spirit of love for the past, a love of our traditions, our people, our heroes, our history, and our literature. The Jewish home might very well be termed the fortress of the future. We must revive the spirit of the home and restore the altar of our faith. We must turn back the hearts of the children to the parents. We must make the home a *mikdash*, a dwelling permeated with moral and ethical living.

"Correct thy son," advises King Solomon, "and he will give thee rest; yea, he will give delight unto thy soul." We must make a spiritual counter-attack. We must decrease the emphasis on making a "fast buck." We must once again talk about integrity, honor, dedication. Remember, moral values are taught, not caught. The home must once again become the school where character is developed, where lessons in moral living are observed. This is the antidote to our present moral collapse.

CHAPTER TWENTY-FOUR

What Do You Give Your Child?

THE other day, a grandmother remarked to me, "I raised two daughters and six sons on stories about my life in a small town in Poland. I told them that in the old country people were measured in only one way; either they had hearts or they didn't. Their wealth or lack of it, their power or their weaknesses were seldom mentioned. Such things didn't matter too much."

"What mattered in those days," continued the grandmother, "was character. This was stressed in the home. Children were taught to understand and appreciate the value of responsibility, hard work, and community living. They knew they were *part* of a family, not the family itself."

This alert, active, vibrant grandmother did an excellent job in raising her family. All are respected members of the community. All have found places for themselves in social and economic circles. All have families of their own. All understand what it means to live as part of a group.

Things are a bit different today. Now, when a parent is confronted with his son's failure, he recalls the material blessings lavished on the child and bitterly complains, "But we give him just about everything. He has an ample allowance, his own room, his own radio and television set, a well equipped playroom . . . ."

The parent who claims he gave his child everything is, of course, referring to material comforts. He, unfortunately, omitted to give his child the things he received from his parents. He failed to transmit the legacy he inherited.

Of all the maladjusted children in our society some of the saddest cases are those who receive too much attention from over-anxious parents—parents who give too much too often. I know of a boy of ten who has to be helped with his dressing every morning. I know another child who throws tantrums on the parlor floor in order to get attention. I know a mother who hangs over her child's highchair watching every bite the boy takes with unconcealed concern. These children are on the way to many problems.

No mother ever intends to favor one child above another, but, human nature being what it is, this sometimes happens. Jacob is a case in point. He is a talented and brilliant child in a family of five. His brothers and sisters are quite ordinary children. Jacob, however, is given every possible advantage of training and contact with people who might serve to further his progress.

All this has made the brothers and sisters feel like "poor relatives" in his presence. Worse than this is the effect upon Jacob himself. From a lovable boy he is turning into a conceited, self-centered child who thinks the world revolves about him.

Early in life a child should be taught to dress himself. Of course, this takes patience on the part of the mother. Early in life a child should learn that he gets nothing if he throws a tantrum. Quietly but firmly he should be taught that this is the wrong way of getting attention.

It would be effective if the parent inculcated in his children imperatively needed ideals—integrity, honesty, industry, to mention but a few. When you give a child these things, then you really give him everything.

This should be done early in the life of the child. In the formation of character the most important time of a person's life is the first five or six years, while the child is under the constant care and protection of the home. Here it is that character is determined. Neglect during these first few years can never be completely overcome. Subsequent training may correct it in a measure, but its influence can never be obliterated.

Teach your child discipline. The one thing he shouldn't learn is that every time he lifts his voice his mother or father will come running to serve him. Yes, teach your child discipline, but at the same time show him love so that he experiences great warmth. If your child feels you love him, you can be extremely strict. However, if you are non-loving or non-giving; if your youngster feels you do not love him very much, that you are unfair, or that your discipline is strictly a matter of your comfort rather than his training, he will resent even the slightest discipline.

One of the most important ingredients in the shaping of a child's personality is the personality of his parents. The surest way to have a happy child is to see to it that he has happy parents. The best assurance for a well-adjusted child is to have well-adjusted parents. If the parents are happy with each other, the climate for personality growth will be good.

Children grow in an emotional climate. They breathe in air but at the same time absorb attitudes, fears, hates, loves, and tensions. They cannot be taught love while we adults practice hate. They cannot be taught to be calm while we spout our wrath. We must remember that feeling and attitudes are not taught to children, but are rather caught by them. If we cultivate friends because we genuinely like them, rather than because of what they can do for us, our children will, too. If we reward good service with praise and not just with a factual acceptance, our children, too, will work to please as well as to be paid. If we follow what we honestly believe to be right and not merely because it is popular, our children will have the courage to think independently. Every noble deed springs from a character that has been trained in small things. A child's character is the complete sum of all his thoughts and all of what he has observed about him, generally in the home. A home is hardly a home unless it contains vitamins for the mind and soul, as well as for the body.

The best tonic in life is a sense of security, but it must be understood that a sense of security is no accident of birth. It cannot be injected in the same way that an anti-polio shot is. It cannot be taken in capsules or pills, as vitamins are. Children are not empty bottles to be filled. They are alert, sensitive individuals who reach forward eagerly or recoil quickly, depending on the understanding of the adults around them.

The child who has achieved a successful relationship with his parents, who has friends to turn to, and who has learned how to control his emotions, will be in a better position to make decisions and will not feel wrecked by a failure or disappointment. He will understand that even in the happiest of lives, some failure is inevitable. He will enjoy his work. He will offer love. He will understand imperfections in others because he realizes his own inadequacies. He will adjust himself to his environment. If he suffers from some inferiority, he will at least attempt to change what he finds to be an intolerable situation. There are shocks in this tense world of ours, shocks that may worry a child, make him somewhat unhappy—but if he has been raised in the proper emotional climate, he will be basically secure. The emotional weather may not always be calm, but in a good climate, trees grow sturdy enough to withstand an occasional storm.

Children are wonderful. They are the wholesome part

of the race. They are pure, adventurous, honest, frank. They are unspoiled. They are eager and are alive with every fibre in their body. They want to learn and are curious about things adults take for granted. They ask questions, thousands of them, and expect answers.

They are ingenious, mischievous, greased lightning. They fill the earth with joy, kindness and good humor. They help us keep young. They bring back to us memories of our youth. They give real meaning to our lives. Through them we can achieve eternal life. Need we repeat that children have been entrusted by God to our keeping? It is our duty to present to them a world that is good and that will reward their interests, their pursuits and their thoughts. These very children today, these perpetual bits of atomic energy, will some day be our great scientists and surgeons, our jurists and rabbis, our leaders in government. Today they fill our lives; tomorrow they may well save them.

A wonderful story is told about children.

"Don't you have any homework tonight?" a father asked his third grade son, whose eyes were glued to the TV set.

"Sure," replied the son without turning his head from the screen, "but I got all my work done in school."

"Well then," the parent persisted, "have you studied your *Chumash*? Tell me, why did God make you?"

The young boy hesitated, but not for long, "God made me," he said simply, "because He likes kids."

CHAPTER TWENTY-FIVE

As You Receive Your Diploma

SOME time ago, a rabbi and a soap manufacturer went for a walk together. As they walked along the city streets, the manufacturer turned to the rabbi and asked: "Rabbi, of what value is religion? After thousands of years of teaching about goodness, truth, honesty, respect—after all the prayers offered and sermons preached, there still is so much trouble and misery in the world. If religion is beneficial, why should this be?"

The rabbi continued walking as he mulled the question over in his mind. Soon they reached a crowded street filled with boys and girls playing in the gutter. Many of them were filthy with sweat and grime. The rabbi, pointing to one particularly dirty child said, "Look at that child. He is about the dirtiest youngster I've ever seen. You say that soap makes people clean but you can almost peel the dirt off that boy. What good is soap? With so much soap in the world, the child is filthy. I question the effectiveness of soap!"

The manufacturer, protesting, stopped in his tracks and said: "That's not fair, Rabbi, soap can't do any good until it is used!"

"This is just the point," replied the rabbi. "So it is with religion. It too is not effective unless it is used!"

It is this, more than anything else, that makes a mockery of religion. We cannot say, "We believe in the Ten Commandments" and at the same time fail to live by them. Imagine what would happen to our society, if those who

believe in the Ten Commandments would really live by
them for twenty-four hours. What a moral revolution
would ensue! Belief and moral action are indivisible. To
believe without proving belief through our deeds is an
admission of moral weakness.

There is much that can be told you today. There is a
world of activity ahead of you. You must do, work, create,
hope, study, learn, and be useful to your people. Our sages
have said, "There are three crowns—the crown of Torah,
the crown of priesthood, and the crown of kingdom, but
the crown of good behavior stands above all."

Rabbi Joshua ben Levi took a trip to Rome. He was
astounded to behold the magnificence of the buildings, the
statues covered with tapestry to protect them from the
heat of the summer and the cold of winter. As he was
admiring the beauty of Roman art, a beggar plucked at
his sleeves and asked him for a crust of bread. The rabbi
looked at the statues, and turning to the man covered with
rags, cried out: "O Lord, here are statues of stone covered
with expensive garments. Here is a man, created in Thine
own image, covered with rags. A civilization that pays more
attention to statues than to men shall surely perish."

So, speak not evil of anyone and do not hurt your
neighbor. Gain his love and respect. Remember that good
behavior and honest actions are the cement which unites
and strengthens humanity. All of us can give friendship
to those who need it, loyalty to those who depend upon us,
courtesy to all those with whom we come in contact, kindness to those whose paths may cross ours, understanding to
those whose views may not be in accord with our own.
We must build up the other person, make him feel important. The world is in need of just this. If you make the
next person feel he is worthwhile, he will see you in the
same light. The prayer of each of you may well be: "Lord,

give me the courage to change what can be changed; the patience to bear what cannot be changed; the wisdom to tell one from the other."

Take the words of Rabbi Amiel to heart. "He who is silent is forgotten, he who abstains is outdistanced, crushed; he who ceases to grow greater, becomes smaller; he who leaves off, gives up; standing still is the beginning of the end."

The yeshivah graduate knows he is a human being, created in the image of God. He is not, as has been defined in a college text-book, "An ingenious assembly of portable plumbing." To the yeshivah graduate, life should be a partnership with God. This then is the central message to the boys who are getting their yeshivah diplomas. Man is man because there is something Divine in his existence. This is why human life is holy.

What does God want of you? He wants your life to be a song. He has written the music for you in His Decalogue and in the duties that come to you in your everyday life. The things you ought to do are the notes set on the staff. To make your life give forth beautiful music, you must live in a way that is pleasing to God. Remember, any action contrary to His teaching is like the singing of a false note. It yields only discord.

A young man once found a dollar bill while crossing a street. From that time on he never lifted his eyes from the ground while walking. In the course of 40 years, he accumulated 29,516 buttons, 52,375 pins, 22 pennies, a counterfeit half-dollar, assorted keys, a drooping head, a bent back, and a miserable disposition. He lost the glories of the light, the smiles of his friends, the songs of birds, the beauties of nature, and varied opportunities to serve God and his fellow-man. Not only did he waste his youth, he failed to prepare for his later years.

As a student of the secular world, you've read about the great advances made in the past 70 years. You've read about the advent of aviation, the invention of the talking movie as well as radio and television. You've observed the mechanization of the farms and the electrification of homes. You have learned about the automation of industries and the building of new industrial centers. You have been taught the miracles of a new chemical age and the conquest of deadly disease. You have seen the life span of the individual lengthened. You realize that man has learned to swim under water like a fish and to fly in outer space like a bird. All that now remains for him to do is to learn to walk this earth like a human being. Progress has been made mechanically, scientifically and chemically. Unfortunately, too little progress has been made in humanity, understanding, and brotherly love. In every corner of this frightened world, there is bloodshed and threatened annihilation. What a society we live in! A society where we set one day aside and call it Mother's Day, one day we call Father's Day, one week we call Brotherhood Week, and one entire month we dedicate as *National Tavern Month.*

In our present society it appears that greater emphasis is placed upon beer than on bread; upon the dollar sign than on the Star of David; on gambling than on God; on hormones than on the home; on the liquor business than on the business of the Lord; on saloons than on salvation; on the stomach than on the soul; on Saturday as a holiday than on *shabbat* as a holy day; on taxes than on truth.

Now that you have your diplomas, grow and mature. Pray that you will be big enough to admit your shortcomings honestly; brilliant enough to accept flattery modestly; tall enough to tower above deceit; strong enough to understand human frailties; wise enough to recognize your errors; humble enough to appreciate greatness; loyal enough to stand by your friends; human enough to be thoughtful of your neighbors; and righteous enough to be devoted to the love of God.

For your sake was the world created. In *Bereshit*, we learn that a single man was created in the world, in order to teach that if any man has caused a single soul to perish, Scripture considers it as though he had caused the whole world to perish. But if man saves a single soul, Scripture considers it as though he had saved the whole world.

Let first things come first. First do good deeds, and then ask God for greater knowledge. First act righteous and upright, and then ask God for wisdom. First grasp the way of humility, and then ask God for understanding.

It is said there are seven hundred thousand words in the English language. Of course, learn as many of these words as you have time to learn, but be certain that you know that the

Greatest word	is God,
Longest word	is Eternity,
Swiftest word	is Time,
Nearest word	is Now,
Darkest word	is Sin,
Meanest word	is Hypocrisy,
Deepest word	is Soul,
Strongest word	is Education,
Dearest word	is Parent, and the
Most meaningful word	is Torah

CHAPTER TWENTY-SIX

Jewish Youth On Vacation

WITH a hug and a kiss, with a pat on the back, with last minute pleas for lengthy letters, the parent fondly bids good-bye to his child and watches him eagerly board the bus or train for summer camp. The scene takes place thousands of times, because summer and day camps have become big business. Tremendous amounts of money are poured into advertising the special facilities and programs that each camp features. All seem to stress the development of the child's athletic and recreational habits.

"We have a private lake and a filtered pool," advertises one camp.

"We have professional clay tennis courts," boasts a second.

"Our program includes archery and riflery," states a third.

"We teach dramatics, music, arts and crafts, and *Chumash*," promises a fourth.

The perplexed parent, wishing to do the best for his child, cannot seem to select the camp most suitable to his child's interests. The maze of colored snapshots, 16mm. movies, and expensive brochures has left him confused.

While there is no doubt that the physical facilities in a camp are important, the parent must be aware that the philosophy of the camp program is far more important. Just as similar vitamins are not helpful to all people, so camps do not fit all campers. Some children do not belong in a sleeping-in camp. Some belong in a hotel-day-camp. Some belong at home wth their parents.

Selecting the proper camp for a child is of vital importance to a parent. It must be remembered that boys and girls spend about one thousand hours in school during a school year; whereas a camper spends nearly *fifteen hundred consecutive hours* in a summer camp. The influence of a summer camp cannot be minimized since it is an important factor in the character and personality development of the camper. It should be utilized to help youth find stability within themselves.

If the child is not to be confused, if the growth of his religious attitude toward spiritual and eternal values is to keep pace with the broadening of his mind, if the boy or girl is to gain maturity with a strong and intelligent faith in God, then he must be placed in a healthy religious environment during the summer. If schools help shape our nation's leaders, as we are often told, how much influence can a summer camp exercise in the religious training of our youth.

The orthodox parent, who selects a "kosher" camp, must be made aware that sometimes this "kosher" camp is not what the rabbi ordered. The word too often applies only to the physical facilities of the camp—two sets of dishes, kosher food, Friday and Saturday services. It by no means indicates that the camp boasts of an orthodox approach to religion. The parent, too often, sterilizes what the child places into his mouth, but does not immunize him against non-orthodox viewpoints practiced in some camps.

There are certain questions the orthodox parent must ask himself. "Will my child's stay in camp conflict with his yeshivah teaching? Will my child's stay in camp present him with serious socio-religious conflicts? Will my child's stay in camp make him question the environment of his

home? Will he doubt the significance of traditions, ceremonies, and customs?"

Orthodox children should only attend genuine orthodox
camps. This type of camp can do a great deal for the child
by offering religion and religious observances in a wholesome atmosphere. It helps build a happy attitude toward
Jewish life. The camper is enthralled by the beauty of the
Shabbat. He watches and joins with his bunk-mates and
counselors in the preparation of the holy day. He attends
daily *minyanim.* He contributes to the charity collection.
He is impressed with the Sabbath ceremonies. He watches
the lighting of the candles, joins in the chanting of the
prayers, listens to the making of the *Kiddush.* His mind is
imbued with the cleanliness, the holiness, the beauty, the
serenity of the day.

On vacation, he lives a full Jewish life. He understands
that God does not take a vacation. He perceives that during
the summer months one can be as devout a Jew as during
the school months. And he learns, yes he does. He learns
more about traditions. He helps examine the camp *"eruv."*
He helps build a *"mechitza,"* a separation. He learns about
the history of his people. He helps organize *"eicha"* services.
He becomes a *Gabbai,* a *Shammos,* a *Chazan,* a Rabbi, during
the course of the summer. He delivers a sermon on the
Sedra of the week. He is, in truth, living Judaism.

A parent must understand that the center of gravity
in religion is not in reading, or in studying, but rather in
doing and living. At camp, the child sees the application of
the principles he learned at school. His religious education
takes on added significance. It awakens in his heart and
mind a greater love for Jewish observance and a greater
understanding for Jewish custom.

The child sees that there is no conflict between being
a traditional Jew and a regular American boy or girl. He

understands that you certainly can be a religious Jew, observing all the principles and tenets of Judaism, and still join in social and athletic events. Look at the life-saving instructor, the hero of the camp. Notice how he sets aside a few hours a day to learn *gemorah*. Look at the tennis instructor. He is in the *smicha* class of the yeshivah.

Religious observance and baseball, Jewish culture and campfires—all are important in the character-shaping of our youth. It is the essence of democracy not only to bring about unity but also to develop the individuality of the person to the utmost possible degree.

So, pick your child's camp with care. Consult your rabbi. Talk to the camp director. Ask him about the camp philosophy. Determine if there are educational classes in the program. In other words, just don't send your child to camp but rather enroll him in a summer athletic, educational, recreational group that is run along orthodox religious lines.

CHAPTER TWENTY-SEVEN

Parents Never Send Bills

W HAT makes a man a good father? In *Kiddushin,* the father's obligations to his son are spelled out: He must circumcise him, redeem him, teach him Torah, teach him a trade, and help him secure a wife. The father who sincerely devotes himself to these duties is a good parent.

Ask a mother the same question and you receive a more detailed answer. She feels there is much more to being a parent than the duties listed in *Kiddushin.* She feels that when a father diapers a child, burps him, bathes him, and helps feed him, he is displaying excellent paternal characteristics. Although there is no reason why a man cannot help occasionally, this alone does not make him a good father.

A father has a distinct role to play in the family. It consists of being a man, a husband, and a male parent. There is a distressing trend in some families for father to become an over-worked handyman, who in his off-duty hours is asked to assume a feminine role in household management—changing diapers, giving bottles, making the formula, feeding the children, running the appliances, taking out the garbage, and doing the weekly shopping. There is evidence in the content of radio programs and comic strips that father, in descending from his male pedestal, has lost his dignity and has become a figure of fun, a lovable, well-intentioned incompetent, who is more to be tolerated than condemned. He is the family provider, who each morning disappears to some vague place called the office.

Some psychologists feel that the process has already gone too far, and that in some versions, the modern father does not give his children a sufficiently clear picture of masculinity; that he is not sufficiently differentiated from the mother to provide a model of manly virtue to his sons. Helping from time to time with the housework is not the same as getting into an apron and wearing it all the time.

Since a father interprets life for a child, he must set a good example of the male of the species. By virtue of interaction with his father, the male child learns how to grow up to be a man, to develop masculine attitudes, to play his role in society.

Some time ago a group of teen-agers were asked to describe virtues they would like to find in fathers. Here are a few worth considering.

"A father should have patience and understanding and should attempt to understand his child's problems. He should find time to devote to him and should participate actively in his life."

"A father should consider a child as an equal member in the family. He should respect the child's privacy, suggest solutions to problems, allow his children to learn slowly and to make their own mistakes."

What a man gives of himself to his children is far more important than how much of it he gives. By actively sharing his life with his children, a father eventually becomes a friend, and the responsibilities of parenthood blossom into the pride of association. A father should realize that if he works upon marble, it will some day perish; if he works upon stone it will eventually crumble to dust; but if he takes a child and trains it well, he will rear a monument which time can never efface. A father must realize that one day his son will follow his example, instead of his advice.

The wise mother will quickly understand that the father belongs at the head of the household and should not be reduced to the status of wage earner only. The wise mother will insist that her husband assume his responsibilities in the raising of the family.

Yet, no home is complete without a mother. In fact the Talmud states, "The home is the temple of the woman, the education of her children is her divine service, and the family is her congregation." Nothing that was ever written can state the role of mothers in better language. At home with her family a woman can do the job for which she was created. One of the greatest Talmudic masters summed up the significance of the Jewish mother when he said that he never called his wife, "wife," but "home."

Children are raised at home. They are not reared at a meeting or a conference. Character is developed at home— at home, where religion is part of the normal pattern of daily life. Character is strengthened where words of Torah re-echo; where the Hebrew *Sefer* is honored, where *Zmirot* are sung. Character traits and habits are implanted in the mind of the child where love and understanding are woven into a child's personality.

A mother must prepare herself for her job in child education. Too long has she been content to sit on the side-lines, with her sole function being to sign the report-card and attend P.T.A. meetings.

Simply stated, children need their mothers. The younger child needs physical attention and the "tender loving care" we hear so much about. This cannot be delegated to a $1.00 an hour baby-sitter, nor to a nursery school, not even an expensive one. The older child needs a wise, friendly, rested listener who will not hesitate when necessary to lay down the firm hand of mature judgment. It is a sad moment in the life of a school child to come home to an empty house, and find his greeting in the form of a note on the kitchen table. A written statement of "love and kisses from Mom" just doesn't take the place of the real thing.

A mother must understand that she is the center and soul of the family, caring for everything, for everyone, and loved and honored by all. By including the honoring of the mother in the Fifth Commandment, and by placing the latter after the hallowing of the Sabbath, Judaism has indicated how important the mother is in the family setup. Mother love carries with it the sweetest joys, the greatest measure of tenderness and devotion. Mother is always on hand to quiet the crying child; to take part for a moment in its play; to give correction and help. She is always on hand to receive the child's confidence. In this way she weaves a daily growing fabric of understanding and of love which will always hold the hearts of her children close to her own.

Education does not begin in the school room, nor does it end there. The mother who is really interested, can play a significant role in the educational development of her child. She certainly can prepare her child for the world of learning. She can help formulate learning habits, and a genuine love for education. She can give her child the interests that will help him in school. Mothers delay too long the teaching of a way of life to their children. They evidently don't realize that a child is never too young to begin training.

Mothers in general are doing a good job in raising their children. Yet, a few words of advice and guidance are in order.

Know and understand your children. Take note of their needs, interests, worries and social problems. Capitalize on their special interests and abilities. Bear in mind, it isn't what happens in the school-room but what happens at home that will help bring out the best of your children.

Help your children to develop a sense of belonging-to-
the-family, instead of the lone-wolf feeling. Attempt to
establish a relationship of mutual respect and confidence.
Try to establish an atmosphere of friendliness without re-
linquishing your authority as a parent. Jewish ceremonies
help keep a family together. The Sabbath and the festivals
are family holidays. *Kiddush, zmirot,* the *Seder,* eating in
the *Succah,* the Purim *Seudah*—all these invest the family
with dignity and give it a feeling of togetherness.

Respect the child's individuality, his thoughts, feelings
and opinions. He is then more likely to respect yours. Avoid
sarcasm, embarrassing remarks, cutting statements. If you
must discipline, do it in private. The Bratzlaver Rebbe advises: "When the parent is quick-tempered, the children
are fools." Use common sense in administering correction,
and overlook minor infractions of home discipline. Follow
through on all your promises, and remember that praise
is better than punishment—love is more potent that hate.

The mother is the teacher in the family. In Exodus
(19.2) we read, "Thus shalt thou say to the house of Jacob,
and tell the children of Israel." That hour when the Torah
was given to us, Moses was bidden to speak first to the
House of Israel, and this referred to the women. Why?
Because it is they who send their sons to school; because
they move their sons' hearts with good words; they watch
over them and teach them to fear sin.

Perhaps a few ideas should be included in regard to
the working mother. The homemaking-working mother will
agree that she is under some strain in her efforts to fulfill
two consuming responsibilities, her home and her job. She
is faced with meeting the needs of her job, her husband,
her children, her home, and her friends. At times her load
is too much for her and somewhere, something gives way,
someone feels neglected.

What advice can be given to working mothers who wish to avoid making errors in raising their children? To begin with, enlist the aid of your children. Patiently, teach them to do a good job. Guide them toward constructive reading habits and purposeful hobbies. Don't leave long daily notes, listing the chores that are to be done. Train them to be as independent as possible. Take time to listen to their tales of the day's experiences. Keep the evening a happy time and at bedtime give each child a bit of private time with you. Make each one feel that no matter how much you are away from home, your love has not been diluted.

Much can happen to the child of a working mother. He may develop a sense of insecurity because he feels he cannot cope with the world's problems by himself. He may get into trouble for want of guidance and direction. Because he is angry with his working mother, he may express destructive and anti-social behavior.

Emotional immaturity is a problem we frequently see in younger children of working mothers. Children who receive too little as well as those who receive too much love have trouble standing on their feet emotionally. Their need for love becomes excessive and it may be manifested in many ways. Lack of attention at home may lead to the use of unacceptable devices for attaining it. A child may seek special care and affection by imagining he is sick or by making much of little.

In spite of hardships, mothers, both working and not, as well as fathers, manifest their love for their children. Father enslaves himself at a job which he often dislikes; mother keeps on with her cooking, cleaning, sewing, worrying—neither of these people entertaining any thought of reward. What torrents of life-force, of goodness, of sacrifice pass from parents to children! Parental love carries with it the sweetest joys—joys mixed with a generous measure of tenderness, devotion, and self-sacrifice. Is it any wonder that the Baal Shem Tov prayed that love of God should be like the love of parents for children?

What do parents do? They create, add beauty and meaning to life. They give new hope to discouraged children and new strength to those who are weak. They help the fallen to rise and start again. They make life seem more worthwhile. Their words, lectures, criticisms, and sermons are indeed benedictions. Is it any wonder that God commanded, "Honor thy father and thy mother, that thy days may be long upon the land which the Lord thy God giveth thee."

Is it any wonder that a mother once turned to her teenage son and asked, "How much does a child cost?"

"Cost!" the boy replied, "Just what do you mean—his shoes, his hat, his bicycle, his wrist-watch, his—?"

"No," replied the pensive mother. "You have it all wrong. The items you mention are really the least expensive. I was thinking of other costs, much greater costs. I was thinking of what agonizing pain and suffering a child costs, what fatigue and watching, how much of a mother's torturing anxiety, how much of a father's toil, how many prayers, fears, and yearnings, how much patience, how much responsibility, how much instruction, how much correction, how much love, how much sorrow, how many lectures, how many sermons, how many sleepless nights. These are the costs I was thinking about, the costs that just cannot be measured in dollars, or counted in material benefits."

If a child only paused to consider, he would then understand that the aggregate costs represent a life-time of giving. He would see a lengthy parade of years filled with continued acts of parental self-denial. He could list the years of material giving—the clothing, feeding and housing, the summers spent at private camps, the private tutors, the special schooling that was his. Unfortunately these every-day items of expenditure are taken for granted by children.

Itemize, if you can, the untold pain and suffering parents experience when a child is ill, or hurt, or in the hospital . . . the sleepless nights, the around-the-clock vigil kept at a child's bedside. Just as every drop of water in an ocean is influenced by the mysterious forces of the tide, so parents feel every pain and every discomfort of a child. Has a scale yet been devised to measure the silent prayers of parents?

Modern children, brought up in this world of stocks and bonds, submit bills for help given to parents. And these children want to be paid promptly and in legal tender. Suppose parents sent bills to children! Now that would be a change! They could be sent daily, weekly, monthly, yearly. There would be difficulty in their preparation. What items should be included? Which expert could appraise the amounts to be listed?

Fortunately, parents never send bills. They give with-out any thought of ever collecting.

CHAPTER TWENTY-EIGHT

Lessons That Haven't Been Taught

WISELY does *Midrash Mishle* caution parents, "If you do not bend the twig of a vine when it is young, you cannot bend it when it hardens." Children build their character and personality by the bricks of habit they pile up day by day. If parents and teachers wish to avoid sowing seeds of laziness in the young, they must instill self-confidence and a proper attitude toward work and duty. With this in mind, children, as far as possible, should have an environment in which they feel happy and yet not frustrated. They should have discipline and instruction to the degree that their abilities warrant, a good deal for the able, and somewhat less for the less able. "He who rebukes not his son leads him into delinquency," is the advice found in *Shemot Rabbah*.

There is one lesson that children have learned well. They know all about what society and parents owe them. They have a long list of what they consider their sacred rights . . . allowance, private room, freedom from chores, summer vacation. Apparently, a lesson that hasn't been taught, at least so far, is what they owe society and their parents. They know little about responsibility, cooperation with household duties, respect for law, order, and tradition. Teachers and parents too often give of themselves without asking for any repayment. They give everything for nothing. They grant every request without making any of their own. They treat children as if they were the absolute kings and queens in the household.

There was a time when parents were their own authorities about raising children. They were, so to speak, the law-makers, the judges, the jury, and the Supreme Court. Children were supposed to be "seen and not heard." The fear of God and parents was instilled in them. No back talk was permitted and children understood that their parents had the final say. The homes of yesterday were adult-centered with the parent firmly entrenched as the head of the household.

Today, we have the child-centered home where there is unfortunately too little respect for authority. The parent, in his great desire to abide by psychological dictum, "to give tender, loving care," has made the child the master in the home. The whim of the youngster seems to reduce the parent to the role of beggar and servant, who, though catering to every wish, must at the same time beg for obedience. Evidently, parents today are "seen and not heard."

It is time to change the present attitude about the rearing of children. Parents must understand that the home environment of a child may determine his character and personality as an adult. Drs. Spock and Gesell, in their psychological writings about children, set down rules for child training which indicate the need for early habit formation.

The Bratzlaver Rebbe, predating the above authorities, stated his views. With his Hasidic wisdom he taught that "children will be healthy and well-bred, if parents do not indulge them too generously." "Train a child in the way he should go, and when he is old he will not depart from it."

Adults may wreck the character of children, and destroy their lives by poor attitudes, and by over-protection. Everyone knows that a knife cannot be sharpened on silk or muslin. The hard surface of the stone is used. So, too, with a child's intellect and with a child's mind. They are sharpened not with coddling, not with spoiling, not with the things that are easy and convenient, but with the intelligent use of discipline. It is a known fact that children who do what they like when they like to do it are not being taught properly. Before very long, these same children will cease to like what they are doing.

It is up to the parent to teach limits to children and to make the child understand the meaning of discipline. In this regard the Talmud gives an excellent bit of advice: "Do not threaten a child. Either punish or forgive him." Threats indicate parental indecision. Punish immediately and let the punishment fit the wrong committed. Let the child understand that you are not angry with him, but rather with what he did. It is further said that "Anger in a home is like rottenness in a fruit." In Proverbs, we read, "He who spares his rod hates his son, but he who loves him seeks to discipline him."

Saadia Gaon offers three methods of teaching children. The first and weakest consists in saying to the one to be taught: "Do this: do not do that," without making him understand the consequences of the command or the prohibition.

The second kind consists in giving, together with the command or prohibition, the consequences of the path chosen. Thus: "Do this, and you will be rewarded: do not do that, or you will be punished." This method is better than the former, for it awakens the idea of happiness or of misery resulting from the path of conduct chosen by the individual.

The third kind of education, while it consists in giving command and prohibition, and in indicating the recompense or punishment that will follow, adds the history of those people who have obeyed and were rewarded and of those people who disobeyed and were punished. This method is most effective since it tests and adds experience to the commands, and to emphasize the lesson, brings in the personal testimony of those who were rewarded and those who were punished.

This is the type of lesson all children understand, and for that matter adults as well. Adults are aware of the exact penalties that will be set when they violate certain traffic rules. The blue ticket tied to the windshield of the car not only lists the offense but the penalty to be paid. There is no doubt that knowledge of the penalty deters many drivers from violating the law.

There is no greater gift an adult can give a child than a proper preparation for life. With such a gift in the beginning, the child is forever enriched. He will use it every day of his life as long as he lives. It is a gift that grows with use. Home, father and mother constitute the first impressions of the child. These three place their seal upon his future character and personality. "The child is a young sapling," write the rabbis (*Midrash Rabba* 22) "and a parent's task is similar to that of a gardener. They must tend the child and see that the young sprout has enough sunlight and sufficient water and air and that the choking weeds are removed from him. It is well to remember the words of the scholar who wrote, 'Train children in their youth, and they won't train you in your old age.' "

Children will be children if only adults will permit them. Children want discipline and adults give them license. Children love roughness and adults give them ease. Children crave activity and adults create idleness for them. Why should children walk when we make it so easy for them to ride? Why should they stand when they can sit? Why should they show respect for their parents and teachers when it is not demanded of them? The Bratzlaver Rebbe was right when he remarked, "We have the kind of children we deserve."

We cannot afford to make things too simple for our children. This is no preparation for life's difficulties. Childhood can be compared to basic training. In this regard Rabbi Leib Pistiver observed: "When a child is taught to walk, his parents hold his hand at first; then they allow him to walk alone, but stand nearby; then they go further and further away from him, until at last the child becomes accustomed to walk steadily on his own feet."

Children are supposed to be mature enough to accept some of the weight parents have carried for years. For years parents have nursed, protected, helped, appealed, begged, excused, tolerated, and denied themselves needed comforts so the children could have every benefit. This they have done gladly, for children are their dearest treasure. But children have no right to expect them to bow to every whim and fancy just because selfish ego instead of common sense dominates their personality, thinking, and requests.

Parents must stop running from their children. They have a right to live. If not now, when? A humorist once remarked, "When I was young my parents told me what to do; now that I am old, my children tell me what to do. The question I have is, 'When will I do what I want to do?'"

When a child asks, "What can I do? Where can I go?" The answer should be, "Go home. Wash the dishes. Vacuum the floor. Dust the furniture. Hang the stormwindows, plant seeds, paint the woodwork, polish the silverware, rake the leaves, hoe the lawn, sweep the walk, wash the car, scrub the floors, learn how to cook and bake, repair the sink, build a wagon, run errands, get a part-time job, help the rabbi, visit the sick, assist the poor, study your lessons, and then when you are through—and not too tired—read a book." Children owe the world something. They owe it time and talent so that no one will be at war, or in poverty, or sick and lonely again. Children want rights! Give them rights, together with an equal amount of responsibilities. The scales must be balanced.

A child is like a field of corn planted by the hand of a farmer. It must be cultivated and cared for; and if weeds grow in it, or if birds attack the young corn, we cannot expect the field of corn to clear itself. The harvest will be in proportion to the hand that cares for it, neither less nor more.

Most parents agree that the above is true but they are a bit confused at the way children should be handled. They plead for uniform practices that can be followed in the same manner as printed directions on packaged goods. Unfortunately, or fortunately for society, children are different. They are not mass-produced on some factory assembly line. They have different likes and dislikes. They tackle problems in their own way.

A rabbi once said that a great number of children are like wheel-barrows—not good unless pushed. Some are like canoes—they need to be paddled. Some are like kites—if you don't keep a string on them they fly away. A few are like a good watch—open face, pure gold, quietly busy and full of good works.

Know your child. Push him, paddle him, keep a string on him. Praise his good qualities—but compel him to carry his own weight in life.

CHAPTER TWENTY-NINE

Doctor, Can You Recommend
Readings in Child Guidance?

JUVENILE delinquency is on the increase. Marriage has been called the great American failure. Many couples who present a unified front to the world are, in reality, living in what a serious humorist called "holy deadlock." There is a moral crisis facing the nation. Parents are in a panic. Educators are troubled. Government agencies are probing into the distressing situation. There are committees, subcommittees, boards, bureaus, forums, symposiums; all meeting, hoping that reports ultimately will be issued which will help the panic-stricken parent.

Of course, psychologists, psychiatrists, child guidance counselors, psychoanalysts, testing agencies have entered the picture. They interview, test, write books, and rewrite them.

"Be permissive," advises one school of thought.

"Punish the child whenever necessary," states another.

"Be the head of the family," urges a third.

"Don't have a parent-dominated home," claims a fourth.

The confused parent seems to be drowning in a sea of thousands of books and tens of millions of words. He goes from adviser to adviser, from lecture to lecture, adding to his total confusion. He becomes the permissive parent, the dominating parent, the praising parent and the critical parent. He studies with his child, then permits his child to study by himself. He over-protects the child, then allows the child to shift for himself. The child in this situation is a little like a passenger in an automobile, who suffers acutely when the driver is over-anxious, but is relaxed and cheerful when the driver knows what he is doing.

There is a wealth of information available to parents on how to raise children. There is expert guidance on hand to advise the young man and woman contemplating marriage. The advice, though written thousands of years ago, is up to date. In fact, because it has withstood time, it has gained in importance. The advice did not emanate from any psychological school. Freud, Adler, Jung, Horney cannot claim to be the authors. The books referred to are those of Jewish wisdom and Jewish learning. The authors are great rabbis and teachers.

The psychiatrist advises one to be careful in selecting a mate.

The Talmud offers some mighty important steps to be considered before marriage. "Hesitate in selecting a wife. . . . Husband and wife should look upon each other as partners in life. . . . Disparity in ages does not make for a successful marriage. . . . Love your wife as yourself, honor her more than yourself, lead your sons and daughters in the right path."

The psychiatrist advises that the home is important in developing personality and character.

The basis of Jewish life is the family, and the wife is given a prominent place in the household. Her influence on character development is stressed. Our rabbis tell us: "It is related of a pious man who was married to a pious woman that being childless, they divorced one another. He went out and married a wicked woman and she made him wicked. She went out and married a wicked man and made him righteous. It follows that all depends upon a woman."

Joel, son of Abraham Shemariah, laid down a success-

ful therapeutic formula on home environment that we would
do well to follow. "Your home," he said, "must be the
abode of quietude and happiness; no harsh word must be
heard there, but over all, must reign love, amity, modesty,
and a spirit of gentleness." If we followed this advice, our
children might develop a sense of security and adequacy and
might understand and respect one another. They would
understand that everyone lives in a community and not in
a vacuum.

In regard to the duties of a father, much has been written
in our good books. Moses Hasid, in his will, said, "A father
must guard himself against hasty temper in his treatment
of his children. It is a wise habit not to reprove a child
immediately on the offense. It is better to wait until the
irritation has been replaced by serenity." Judah, son of
Saud Ibn Tibbon, about 1150, advised his own son as follows, "My son, devote thy mind to thy children, as I did
to thee; be tender to them, instruct them." It seems that
both these men were excellent guidance counselors in their
day. We have not as yet improved on their advice. We still
caution parents to treat their children with care, to devote
time to them, to help them with their studies.

The psychiatrist says, teach your children by example.

The Vilna Gaon, years ago, urged, "When you lead your
sons and daughters in the good way, let your words be
tender and caressing, in terms of discipline that win the
heart's assent. . . . Accustom them to a life of virtue and
noble character, to which end much training is required.
Habit dominates all things."

The psychologist today advises a parent to discipline
his child. "A pat on the back," says the psychologist, "is
good for a child provided it is done often enough, low
enough, and hard enough." Proverbs, Chapter XIV states:

"He that spareth his rod hateth his son. But he that loveth him chasteneth him betimes."

And so to the question, "Doctor, can you recommend some good readings in child guidance?", I answer, "Yes, most definitely yes." I suggest that you read, together with your spouse and family, the *Sedra* of the week. Study Proverbs, discuss Ethics of the Fathers. Go to the original source for help, the original source being the *TORAH*. This is still the best, most complete *guidance manual* ever published.

CHAPTER THIRTY

Let's Watch Television

WHAT programs did you watch last night? Was it Gunsmoke, Mike Hammer, or Have Gun, Will Travel? Perhaps you watched The Untouchables, or thrilled with "The Killer's Kiss," featured on Naked City. Your TV guide, almost any evening of the week, offers you a wide choice of thrillers and killers. A single evening's menu serves you Highway Patrol, Death Valley, Sheriff of Cochise, Bat Masterson, Tombstone Territory, Scotland Yard, Wagon Train, Hong Kong, San Francisco Beat, Hawaiian Eye, Policewoman Decoy, Johnny Midnight, Tales of the Texas Rangers, Wanted, Dead or Alive, Skid Row, Decoy, Tales of the Falcon, and the Californians. If you are interested in statistics, you might sit with pen and pad some evening and keep score of the number of people shot, stabbed, hung, poisoned, burned, or otherwise sent to the great beyond.

The most horrifying psychological aspect of all this violence in entertainment is that we watch it with complete indifference. We see individuals done away with on the TV screen as we sit munching popcorn, eating ripe grapes, or slowly sipping a cup of piping hot coffee (43 beans to the cupful). We admit characters into our living rooms via the TV screen that we would never dream of permitting through the front door.

We live in a strange world, where 60% of the murders committed in this country are never solved; where the threat of the BIG BOMB is a threat to every human being; where there is danger that a push of a button could blow up the whole planet. Since we live in a world where we experience an all-pervasive anxiety because of violence and threat of violence, it would seem that we ought to shun the mystery story. Yet, this type of program is most popular. Why?

It is true that mankind, ever since brother Cain slew brother Abel, has had to live with the threat of war. But until now, war at least served a function in that it was the ultimate point of decision in an argument between two contestants. When there was no higher court of appeal, two clans or two nations would fight it out. The side that won was right, and life went on. But in a future war, no one can look forward to winning, since everyone will be destroyed.

Yet, we watch these thrillers and read crime stories over and over again, like a neurotic with a repetition compulsion. We seem to believe that if we can see the *"good"* guys triumph over the *"bad"* guys again and again, somehow our own fears will be overcome, our own anxieties will be worked out, and our own tensions will be relieved. It makes us feel more secure to think that the "bad" guys will always be caught, and that our way of life will not be destroyed by some person throwing a bomb. As individuals we feel impotent: what can we do about organized crime or mass murder? But Sam Spade and Mike Hammer can be depended upon to cast out the devils around us.

Unfortunately for us, however, relying on these "saviours" in the entertainment world traps us in a vicious circle, because this is not a real solution to the problem of violence in the world around us. We get caught in the repetition compulsion of frustration, impotence, and anger. We are frightened by our inability to cope with the forces around us. It is this fright that causes us to escape to the wonderful world of the western, the thriller, the mystery story, where the "Private Eye" (very often our own self-image) becomes the hero and overcomes all evil. We flee to TV programs, paper-back mysteries, movie thrillers and comic books for a solution. Tragically enough, we get no real help from that quarter at all.

What we need is faith—faith is the eternal tranquilizer that has brought peace to men's hearts in the presence of life's most awesome tribulations. We need faith in ourselves, faith in our family, faith in our country, faith in God. Faith in a human being is what roots are to a tree. Great oak trees have great roots. Great souls have great faith. The man with faith has confidence in himself, as well as a recognition that God can transform a life.

So next time you turn the dial on the TV set to a murder mystery, ask yourself why? Question the reasons for your inviting into your living room a gang of cutthroats, drunks, evil-looking perverts. Analyze your fears. Question your choice. Determine the need for this type of program. In the final analysis, only you can solve your own fears and conquer your own difficulties.

CHAPTER THIRTY-ONE

– Your Mother and Mine

FROM the dependency of infancy to the dignity of maturity, children are under your influence. Very often the first word a child utters is "mother."

You come in different sizes, enjoy many things, share varied interests. You are found in every country in the world, and there is more than rumor to indicate that you inhabit God's celestial domain. Though you speak different languages, you are united in one goal: to help each child reach the highest degree of individual development.

You are a composite person. You have the energy of Samson, the efficiency of Joseph, the memory of Rashi, the understanding of Aaron, the wisdom of Solomon, the kindness of David, the patience of Job, the modesty of Moses, the nerves of Daniel, the warmth of Sarah, the loyalty of Rebecca, the devotion of Rachel, the love of Leah, the faith of Hannah, and the courage of Esther.

You are an inspiration to poets, a model for artists, the prayer of soldiers, God's messenger to children. To the writer you are the theme, to the philosopher the ideal, to the world the symbol of goodness.

You defied Pharoah, defeated Haman, waged war against Sisera, sacrificed seven sons to God, lived in loneliness for twenty-four years so that your husband could learn Torah, and gave up wealth, security and position for Judaism.

You are the greatest influence in your home, the center and soul of your family. Your heart is the child's schoolroom. You represent love, security and understanding. You are a symbol of all that is right. You have beauty, skill and grace. There is no velvet so soft as your lap, no rose so lovely as your smile, no friendship so pure, so devoted.

You are the source of good deeds and thoughts, the core of spiritual endeavors, the confidante of all undertakings. You give help without becoming a crutch, direct your children without stifling their growth, offer sympathy without smothering. You enjoy the satisfactions, the delights and the pleasures of childhood, yet at the same time understand the griefs, irritations, embarrassments and frustrations of the young.

The most amazing thing about you, the thing that makes you different from any person in the universe, is that you will not entertain the idea of changing jobs with anyone in the world. In fact, you are thankful to God for having entrusted His children to you. Only you are destined to be immortal. "For your sake," teaches the Talmud, "for the sake of the mothers who kept faith in God alive in the hearts of their children, was Israel delivered from Egypt." Is it any wonder that Solomon proclaimed in Proverbs:

You stretch out your hand to the poor; yea, you
    reach forth your hands to the needy.
Strength and dignity are your clothing; and
    you laugh at the time to come.
You open your mouth with wisdom; and the law of
    kindness is on your tongue.
You look well to the ways of your household, and eat
    not the bread of idleness.
Your children rise up, and call you blessed; your
    husband also praises you.
Many daughters have done valiantly, but you
    excel them all.

And years pass. They fly by as children mature and parents grow older. Wedding anniversaries follow one another. Children now have their own families. They have become mothers and fathers themselves. They have sons and daughters, their parents have become grand-parents and great grand-parents. And now the time has come for the Golden Wedding. Here is what a son writes:—

Dear Mom and Dad:

While making plans for the celebration of your 50th wedding anniversary, your children have recalled many incidents concerning our home and upbringing. These are some of my random thoughts on the meaning of this half-century milestone of marriage.

A scientific wit, while in a sentimental mood, once said "Marriage is three portions of love and seven portions of forgiving each other's sin." That's a pat formula and belongs in a laboratory where results must be accurately predicted. This formula certainly did not help the young man who was having a difficult time with his wife during the first few years of his marriage. A well-known humorist tells of such a man who attended a golden wedding celebration and could not help but wonder how two people could stay happily married for fifty years. He finally mustered enough courage to ask the elderly "bridegroom" if he had ever thought of divorce during the 50 marital years. The old man thought for a moment and answered, "Divorce—never; Murder—many times." Seriously, however, marriages can never maintain a level course. We must have our good and bad times and the well-matched mates will work together to see things through the difficult times because of their feelings, not only for each other, but also for what they have made—their home, their partnership, and their children.

The Planning Years—I often wonder how you did it. Certainly you did not use your adolescent years to read what our scholars have written about marriage. Is it easier for the young folks of today? They have such books as *Courtship, Your Dating Days, She's Off to Marriage,* etc., all intended to teach you how to select the partner with whom you will create your family unit, and how to develop attitudes that lead to a happy and successful marriage. Didn't you read any of these books, Mom? If you didn't, then how were you able to build your family so well?

The Early Years—Did you ever read any of the books we have on the methods of raising children? Did you have a "marriage manual" at home? Did you take any courses on child care, family psychology, guidance or homebuilding? Did you read *The Nursery Years* or *The Mother's Guide* or *The Care and Feeding of Children?* You didn't have the time, because you were too busy doing what you thought mothers should do for their children.

The Middle Years—This is just about the time I became aware of the family responsibilities of children and parents. My recollections of these years revive incidents of many kinds. I remember how greatly concerned you were with our progress in school. Any ideas of leaving school for early employment were quickly disposed of with some sort of brief and effective punishment. "You can lose your money many times over but your education is yours to keep." How many times did you say that? My teachers were always right and the school was most important in our lives. We all celebrated the end of the term not only because it meant the start of vacation but because it was promotion day and we earned promotion to the next grade. As a matter of fact, we had to earn practically everything or else we just did without it. Nothing came easy, neither to you nor to us. I also recall some scenes of bloodless warfare at home when you objected to certain friends of ours, and we just refused to understand your point of view. Or when you insisted that our chores at home be completed before we were allowed to go out to play. How tyrannical I thought you were then. I remember that your parties and celebrations never lacked lustre because of financial stress. You seemed to enjoy making these events possible. Now where did you learn to create an environment like that? In looking back to the methods you used in building your family, I wonder if all the books on the subject are necessary. Is it possible that by the time parents find the need to refer to what has been written concerning their homes and children, it's too late?

The Golden Age—And so you reached the time when your children no longer live with you, and are occupied with their own families. We have the advantage of broadcasts, telecasts, movies, books, clubs, lectures, camps, to advise us on family matters. What do you do, now that you don't have to care for children. You are not "The Old Folks at Home" because you have taken on other responsibilities to occupy your leisure time. If being old is a state of mind, then I am older than you are because your interests have increased to a point where you have very little time left for recalling days gone by. You have many new friends, you belong to several organizations—you don't have the time to grow old. These are the golden years when you can, and are, reaping the rich rewards of experience and the wisdom that comes with age.

I think I know your secret. One marriage begets another and the effects of inbreeding must be remembered. Two people, just married, decide not to be concerned with personal needs until the needs of the mate are satisfied. Doing things for others continues after the children come, so that they grow up in an environment where every member of the family is concerned with the next one. We are not neglected, because the family does not allow it to happen. Our needs are met—but without demanding it. It may take a bit longer but it tastes better—and we learn the meaning of love in its real sense. It isn't necessary to read a book to learn the correct thing to do. You just have to want to do it—and you wanted to.

And so I'll end as I started. In a few days we will attend the celebration of your Golden Wedding but I wonder who has more reason to celebrate, you or I? What have these 50 years meant to you and what have they given me? Is it really better to give than to receive? Is there any other place that provides as much comfort and encouragement as a home? Where else but in a home can you find a group of people with a common purpose, towards which each one makes a contribution? Where can you find pleasures equal to the joys of a happy home? For the kind of home you have given us, we are forever grateful; so let us celebrate together. Your loving son. . . .

Mothers get older. Time and spent energy demand their pay. You look at Mom and she seems older in face, though young in spirit. She tires more quickly, though she does not complain. And then one day. . . .

It was Friday at about half past one in the afternoon. Familiar *Shabbos* odors permeated the house. The delicious fragrance of a coffee cake still baking in the oven assailed your nostrils as you came through the kitchen door. Tantalizing whiffs of chicken soup with noodles, prunes and sweet potatoes, compote of peaches and apricots, and a *lokshun* pudding were all keen reminders that soon the "Shabbos Bride" would be welcomed. Ten *challas* were lined up on the kitchen work table. The tempting aroma of freshly cooked *gefilte* fish filled the entire apartment. An embroidered linen cloth covered the table, and six sparkling silver candle sticks, together with a silver wine bottle and wine cups gave an air of spiritual wealth to the table and the home. Everything shone brilliantly, from the carefully scrubbed linoleum on the floor, to the tile on the kitchen walls.

She was not a slave in the "kitchen-world" of most women, but she felt that kitchen was really home, all other rooms being merely necessary annexes. It was in the kitchen that family conferences were held and plans for bar mitzvahs and weddings were made. It was the kitchen that had helped bind the lives of the family together. In the kitchen brothers and sisters and mother and dad exchanged ideas. In the kitchen the family read, dreamt, drank tea, did homework, heard Dad read from the *Sedra* of the week, or Mom relate the latest heart-breaking installment from her favorite column in the *Forvitz*.

There was no doubt that she was a good *balabuste*. Relaxed now, she eagerly could wait for her married children to come for their *Shabbos* bundles. She chuckled with delight as she thought of how delighted her youngest son would be with the specially baked *rogalach* which were his favorite. She glowed with unrestrained joy as she pictured her eldest son eating the potato *kugel* she had prepared for him. She thrilled with enthusiasm because her *challas* would be used for *lechem mishne* in the homes of her *kinder*. "I want them to make a *brocha* over my *challas*," she would often say.

True enough, the children had often pleaded, "Mom, please don't bake and cook for us. We can buy this in the bakery. You're not as young as you used to be. Please conserve your strength."

"Saving my strength this way," she always answered, "would mean sacrificing my greatest pleasure. God should give me strength to bake for you all another fifty years and you should all come here to collect. You have no right to take away a mother's pleasure."

They realized that it was futile to argue with her. If they didn't come (and they had tried that trick once or twice) Pop would be sent by bus, train, or on foot to deliver the *Shabbos* delights. And deliver them he did, more than once.

She was a busy lady, this venerable Jewish mother—her home was like the corner of Broadway and 42nd Street. The telephone never stopped ringing and the door-bell never stopped buzzing. Community problems were her problems. Here was a sick rabbi who needed money to pay medical bills; an old lady who had to be admitted to an old age home; *nadan* was needed to consumate a *shiddach;* matzohs and wine had to be purchased for a poverty-stricken family, or a crib and carriage had to be provided for a new arrival.

And she responded! She dropped all her personal work, gave her time and strength, forgot herself perhaps, but always remembered, "IN DEM ZCHUS VET GOTT ZEIN GUT TSU MEINE KINDER," a phrase she used so very often.

On this particular Friday, she was ecstatically happy. She was going to spend *Shabbos* with one of her sons and so had prepared, in addition to her regular Friday culinary output, *knaidlach,* an onion-*knish,* sweet and sour fish, chocolate and coffee cakes, oat-meal cookies, and an old-fashioned compote. Only lack of traveling space deterred her from preparing a *chulent,* strudel, *kishke,* and other delicacies which she made so expertly. With a twinkle in her eye she said to her husband, "*Oz mi geht tsu a kinde, geht min nit mit ledege hent*—when you visit a child, you don't go empty handed."

Suddenly, without warning, shocking tragedy struck. Time, hard work, extreme pressures, uncontrolled tensions took its toll. A sharp, flashing, agonizing pain in her head transformed this vibrant wonderful mother into a helpless invalid. A paralytic stroke had done its job.

Doctors were called. Children were summoned. Consultations were held.

"Only time will tell," cautioned the doctor.

"Let's say *Tehillim*," whispered the rabbi.

"I don't want to live a single minute without her," sobbed the father.

"Almighty God, please help her, please help Mama, we need her," sobbed the children.

As she fought that night for her life in the hospital, the *challas* she had baked earlier in the day lay unsliced on the *Shabbos* table, the grief-stricken children unable to make a *motze* over them. The joy of the *Shabbos* was clouded.

A series of doctors, specialists, tests, x-rays, consultations followed. For six weeks it was life and death, but she was determined to survive, fighting against all odds.

Doctors, nurses, medical heads all marveled at the "will to live" of this grand mother of ours. That light in her eyes shone brightly. That *ner tamid* in her soul seemed to shout, "I will live, I will live!"

Gamze le tov! God was good. After a long stay in the hospital she was ready to leave for home—paralyzed in body, but alert in mind and spirit. As she was wheeled out on a stretcher to a waiting ambulance, she remarked to her hospital friends, "Pray for me that this hand," pointing to her paralyzed limb, "will some day give charity. God still needs me to do *mitzvos*."

And five additional years passed. Five years of wheelchairs and complete dependence upon others. Five years of praying to God to grant recovery. Five years of thanking God for the many good years He had bestowed upon her and the family. The desire to live was always there. But the strength to fight slowly ebbed. Once again came the hospital bed, and nurses around the clock, and doctors and consultants, and prayers, and hopes, and pleas . . . and, finally, a call to her Heavenly rest. Then came grief, intense grief, grief mixed with gratitude to God for having given her to us for the years of her life.

At this moment of deep hurt, it appears there is no balm for our gaping wounds. We are not amenable to words of consolation. The clouds of grief have cast a thick gloom over our lives. An aching void, an overpowering loneliness, a gnawing pain makes our days dark and unhappy. We have lost what we have had, you, Mama darling, and for this there is no adequate compensation. We are impoverished; our lives have been made poorer. God summoned you to Heaven and left a void in our lives. We sit with anguished hearts as God fondly welcomes you to Heaven amid the jubilation of His angels.

You left your home and family on earth to join your family in Heaven. You left the valley of pain and tears to reach the mountain of peace and joy.

Yet, amidst our grief, if we pause to reflect, we find genuine cause for gratitude—gratitude for the years we had together. The rabbis advised us to think of the good things you did in your lifetime—the charities you founded, the organizations you strengthened, the people you aided, the *mitzvos* you fulfilled, the family you built. As we sat *shiva,* we could think of nothing else, because the years of your life were filled with *ma'asim tovim.*

There is much we can remember; much we can recall. The warm memories, the sustaining influence, the deep roots entwined about us—all these can never be erased by the hand of death. We console ourselves with the happiness we once enjoyed as a complete, undivided, intimate family, and we thank the Almighty that you were ours while we had you.

Ours was not a rich home but it was a happy one. We recall how you used to usher in the holy *Shabbos*. Friday was a day of strain and stress and of tense anxiety; you would rise before dawn, cook and bake and scrub all day long. But it was a labor of love in anticipation of *Shabbos*. We can even now smell the tasty aroma of your freshly baked *challas*, cakes, cookies, and *pletzlach*. And after we were all married, you continued with your baking in even greater quantity. You were the baker and papa was the delivery man for your *Shabbos* delicacies, going to Williamsburg, Kew Gardens, Borough Park, Manhattan Beach, while you sneaked quietly down to the bakery to buy yourself *lechem mishne* for your own *Shabbos* table. When we criticised you for doing this, you smilingly answered, *"Dus iz my gonsa farganigen."*

And Mama darling, you gave us so much in life. Your warm affectionate heart was always brimming with love for your family and carried with it sweet joy, sympathetic tenderness, devotion, and self-sacrifice. It was you Mama who checked our school-work, talked to our teachers, enrolled us in Torah institutions, warmed our hearts with your encouraging words. You gave us, during your lifetime, a spiritual heritage. You gave us a *derech*—taught us *midos, yiddishkeit, menschlichkeit*. You taught us to have faith by holding on to the word of God and to the hand of God. And we can never forget your looking Heavenward and saying, *"Gotenu, Tata zisser, helf meine kinder."*

And darling Mama, we recall how you wanted us to have fun and so took us to parks, playgrounds, and museums. We can remember how you took us on three different trolleys to Coney Island. You played with us, bathed with us. You worked hard but you had time for your children. You shopped, cooked, baked, washed clothes, ironed, made our shirts, blouses and short trousers. You glowed with pride at our small successes. It was you Mama who boosted our egos and planted in us the seeds of adequacy. You had no Gesell, Spock, Adler, Freud; didn't study a handbook on child raising. You raised us by heart; giving us love, attention, care, discipline, and most of all, your TIME.

We remember how you sat in *shul* and prayed. When we were young we dared not look up to the women's section because we could not bear to see your tear-stained face, but we heard your sobbing in your prayers. The entire congregation wept with you as you pleaded with Him on high to be good to your husband and to your children. And Mama darling, when I bent over your hospital bed the day before you died, I heard you say, over and over again, *"Meine kinder zenen my gonsa leiben."* You were dying but you thought not of yourself but of your children. This message of supreme devotion you bequeathed to us.

For years we didn't own a car but that didn't prevent you from going to the chicken market and buying live chickens so that all of us could *shlog kaporos*. You would bring home five live chickens by bus, never for a single moment mindful of the laughter of the fellow passengers.

Never will any of us erase from our minds the scene in our home before we went to *shul* on *Kol Nidre* night. The very walls cried as you lit candles and pleaded with God for another year of health. *"Gotenu,"* you would say, *"kainer fun unz zol nit fahlin, meine kinder zolen mir iber leben."* And then you would call us in, one at a time, to

bless us and pray over us. How you wept when you put
your hands on our heads to give us individual *brochos*.
Mama darling, something precious has been taken away
from us and we think only of what we've lost, how empty
our lives are now. We know we cannot have your prayers
in this way ever again, but we are certain that you in
Heaven, watching over us, will be a *gute beiter* and that
you will pray for papa and us, for your grand-children and
great grand-children.

We remember with modest pride how you went about
selling raffles, theatre tickets, luncheon reservations. Mama,
we used to ruefully reflect that it wasn't safe for us to
bring a friend home because you made certain that he had
purchased some of the charitable merchandise you always
kept in your large, overstuffed, *mitzva*-filled pocketbook.

You walked miles from *shul* to *shul*, addressing groups,
with the buoyant hope that the membership would decide
to support the affair you were sponsoring. And what a
radiant smile you bestowed upon us when you were successful.

We recall how you traveled to the Fulton Fish Market
weekly, going from one dealer to another, asking for dona-
tions. You didn't seem to mind lugging those heavy bags
around all morning, taking them finally to the *Lechem
Ani'im* Society where they were made into food packages
for the indigent. We remember your dedication to the
*Hebrew Ladies Day Nursery, Home of the Aged, Hospital
for Chronic Diseases, Infants' Home, Yeshivah David Leib-
owitz, Chaim Berlin, Toras Emes, Home of the Sages of
Israel, Ladies Auxiliary of the Congregation Agudas Achim
Anshe Sfard*, to mention but a few. You held many offices
in these organizations: President, Chairlady, Member of
the Board of Directors and Board of Governors. You took
your responsibilities seriously. You saw to it that orphans

were fed and housed, and demanded the highest degree of cleanliness. You never asked for honor but only for the opportunity of being helpful. You knew that the measure of a person was not according to the number of his servants but according to the number of people he served. How many times did we hear you say, *"In dem zchus vet mir Gott helfen oz ich vel nit vissen fun kine tzar."*

Your life was a good one. You lived for God, His Torah, His statutes and commandments. You made no compromise with religion. You heard the call of God because you were always within listening distance. You kept on repeating, *"Azoi hot zich mein tata fefiert."* You believed in charity, in helping your fellowman. If a married couple were on the verge of breaking up, you went to make peace, and peace you made. *"Shalom bayis,"* you said, "is a holy *mitzva.*" When a young man and a young woman wanted to marry but had no funds, you arranged the wedding, getting them a house full of furniture as well. *"Hachnosas kalah,"* you advised, "is an important *mitzva.*" When people needed food for Pesach, you made bundles and delivered them personally, so that none needed come begging. *"Maot chitim,"* you whispered, "must be observed." When rabbis needed help, you answered quickly—answered with time, effort, money, heart, dedication. When people had to be saved from Hitler's crematoria, you filled out papers and brought them to this country, making certain first that a home was waiting here for them. And Mama darling, we remember your preparing packages to be sent to Europe; the job you had carrying them to the post office, often having to unwrap and repack them because of some minor regulation.

Mama, we sat listening to the rabbis' eulogies. We couldn't see you but we knew you were with us. You must have heard Rabbi Mirsky say that the Almighty wanted a rose for His Garden, so He plucked you, Rivka. You must have heard Rabbi Twersky, with tears streaming from his eyes, say that you were the spiritual and charitable strength of Brooklyn and that God had lent us a jewel to enjoy and now had reclaimed it. You must have heard Rabbi Schwartz say that your years were full, rich and productive and that you chose to join God when your hands and legs couldn't fulfill the wishes of your heart.

We sit and tears come easily because we have suffered an irreparable loss. The rabbis tell us that life is a loan. "Everything," they say, "is given in pledge to be restored when the Master wills." God's gift to you was a soul which was returned to Him pure and holy. The Kotzker Maggid taught that "Death is merely moving from one house to another and if we are wise, we seek to regard the latter as the abode of beauty."

You have not really left us because so much of you, your hopes, wishes, aspirations, goals, and prayers are in us. The poet wisely says,

> "To live in hearts we left behind
> Is not to die."

You left us a living legacy of wonderful memories. We will keep you alive by following in your footsteps, by living the kind of life you wanted us to live, a life devoted to Torah, *Yiddishkeit,* and to fellow-man. You worshipped God; you understood the discipline of God; learned the truth of God; accepted the will of God; fulfilled the purpose of God; knew the resources of God; realized the power of God; and radiated the peace and love of God. The Talmud teaches that "The righteous are called living, even when they are dead."

Mama darling, may your sacred memory be a constant source of inspiration to all of us.

CHAPTER THIRTY-TWO

Dear Son

THERE is a story told about King Monobaz, who in the days of the Second Temple became a proselyte to Judaism. When a famine took place during his reign, he unlocked his ancestral treasures and distributed his wealth among the poor. His ministers were shocked at this unusual behavior and rebuked him saying, "Thy fathers amassed this wealth; you are squandering it."

"You are wrong," said the benevolent king. "My forefathers preserved earthly treasures, but I preserve heavenly treasures; theirs could be stolen, mine are beyond mortal reach; theirs were barren, mine will bear fruit time without end; they preserved money, I preserved lives. The treasures which my fathers laid by are for this world, mine for eternity."

This story comes to my mind at this time because I hear so much about the responsibility of a father to provide for his children. On every side a parent is bombarded with questions as to how he has provided for his family should he be called away by the Almighty. He is told about the necessity of writing a will, setting up college funds, taking out large insurance policies. All, with the goal of providing for the financial welfare of his family.

It seems to me that a father's obligations go a bit further. Perhaps, when he visits his attorney for practical advice in preparing a "Last Will and Testament," he should also visit his rabbi to secure spiritual advice in the preparation of an ethical will. After all, the will prepared by an attorney distributes money, stocks, bonds, personal property, and real estate. It helps provide for a financial future. It aims to distribute the collected material wealth of a parent. On the other hand, the will prepared by the rabbi bestows upon the heirs a lasting heritage and attempts to offer sincere practical advice about a person's duties and responsibilities. It presents the experience of those who have lived before and have learned from their mistakes. It provides for a spiritual and ethical future.

My son, I am certain that you have come across examples of ethical wills in your studies of Hebrew lore. You who have pored over our *Chumash*, dipped into *Gemorah*, immersed yourself in the study of our commentaries, certainly must be aware of the tremendous amount of spiritual endowments left by our patriarchs and prophets.

A Midrash tells us that Jacob, on his death-bed, gave advice to his sons. He pleaded with the Almighty to stay the hand of the Angel of Death until he had counseled his children. In the 32nd chapter of Deuteronomy, you must have read over and over again, the advice Moses gave to the children of Israel before his lips were sealed forever and his eyes closed. King David, poet and warrior, writer of the Psalms, advised his wise son, Solomon, "I go the way of all the earth. Be thou strong therefore, and show thyself a man; and keep the charge of the Lord thy God, to walk in His way, according to all that is written in the law of Moses, that thou mayest prosper in all that thou doest." David was leaving his son a kingdom but nonetheless felt that parental advice was necessary.

All through history, our rabbis and sages, our men of God, have left ethical wills to their children. My dear son, from this treasure house of experience, from this rich mine of spiritual wealth, I select pearls, the advice of our saintly scholars. There is so much I want to leave you, so much I want you to remember, so much I want you to have.

I'd like to leave you time, years and years of happy, adequate living, and with it my sincere prayers to the Almighty God to make these years full ones; years devoted to the service of God and man. I'd like to bequeath to you the appreciation of God's beautiful world and the thought that one of your greatest possessions is the 24 hours directly ahead of you. I'd like to leave you a strong faith, a treasure of love, and happy memories of your home.

There are so many intangible values that I would like to bestow upon you, my son. A wise man once advised his children to remember twelve things:

> The value of time.
> The success of perseverance.
> The pleasure of working.
> The dignity of simplicity.
> The worth of character.
> The power of kindness.
> The influence of example.
> The obligation of duty.
> The wisdom of economy.
> The virtue of patience.
> The improvement of talent.
> The joy of originating.

To which I would like to add, have clean hands, clean speech, and clean thoughts; stand up for the right against the wrong; work hard and play fair. Pray for forgiveness when you are wrong and forgive those who have wronged you. Help others at cost to yourself, and always remember that you were created in the image of God.

A story is told of a group of men who appeared before the Heavenly Tribunal.

First came a rabbi. "I've studied the law," he said. "Night and day I have pored over the Word of God. I certainly deserve a place in Paradise."

"Just a minute," cried the Recording Angel. "First we must make an investigation to find out what was the motive of your study. Did you apply yourself to learning for its own sake? Was it for the sake of honor, or for mercenary reasons?"

Next came a saintly man. "How I fasted in the life I left behind! I observed all the six hundred and thirteen religious duties scrupulously. I bathed several times a day, and I studied the mysteries of the Zohar ceaselessly."

"Just a moment!" cried the Recording Angel. "We have to make our investigation about the purity of your intentions."

Then an innkeeper approached. He said simply, "My door was always open to the homeless and I fed whoever was in need and hungry."

"Open the Gates of Paradise!" announced the Recording Angel. "No investigation is needed."

My son, charity is a virtue of the heart as well as the hand. Father Abraham was charitable. He sought the weary and tired. His door was never closed. Cherish his way of life as your own. Never turn away the poor who begs empty-handed, even if you can give just a little, for it is said: "Oh, let not the oppressed return confounded." If you have nothing in your possession to give him, then appease him with words. He needs your kindness, your understanding, your sympathy. Do not rebuke a poor man or raise an angry voice against him, for his heart is broken and humble. Crush not the poor with harsh words, for the Lord will plead his cause. Rabbi Ben Azai advised, "Despise not any man, and do not spurn anything; for there is no man that has not his hour, nor is there anything that has not its place."

On holidays, festivals, and Sabbaths seek to make happy the poor, the unfortunate, the traveler who needs your hospitality. Never turn your eyes from the needy and so give him no occasion to curse you; for if he curses you in the bitterness of his soul, his prayer shall be heard of Him that made him. Bear in mind, that those who scatter with one hand, gather with two. Nothing multiplies as quickly as kindness.

My son, I plead with you to do charity and serve others while you are alive. Let me share this illustrative story with you. A rich man once said to a friend, "Why is it everybody is always criticizing me for being miserly, when everyone knows I have made provisions to leave everything I possess to charity when I die?"

"Well," said the friend, "let me tell you about the pig and the cow. The pig was lamenting to the cow one day about how unpopular he was. "People are always talking about your gentleness and your kind eyes," said the pig. "It is true that you give milk and cream, but I give even more. I give bacon and ham—I give bristles, and they even pickle my feet. Still nobody likes me. Why is this?" The cow thought a minute, and then said, "Well, maybe it's because I give while I'm still living."

My son, in many of our synagogues, there is an inscription above the Ark that reads: *"Know Before Whom Thou Standest."* The source of this quotation is the Talmud. Rabbi Eliezer, the teacher of Rabbi Akiba, was once asked by his disciples: "Teach us a way of life." He replied: "Have a constant prayer on your lips that no evil come to anyone through you. And when you pray, know before whom thou standest."

My son, your mother and I have always desired that

you learn to love Torah. It was no sacrifice, but a joy, to
send you to Torah institutions. You added strength to our
souls and years to our lives when you quoted a bit of
Chumash, or *Mishna,* or *Rashi.* We were happy indeed that
you did not consider Torah an inheritance from your
fathers that needed no personal effort to win it. Keep on
applying yourself as you did in your youth. If you do
not toil, you cannot acquire. If you don't learn one day,
you fall behind two days. Always keep in mind, "for the
commandment is a lamp and the law is light."

My son, use your education and wisdom. Rabbi Eleazer
ben Azaryah used to say, "One whose wisdom is greater
than his deeds, what is he like? A tree whose branches are
many and whose roots few. When the wind comes it roots
it up and overturns it on its face. But one whose deeds ex-
ceed his wisdom, what is he like? A tree whose branches are
few and its roots many, so that even if all the winds that
are in the world come and blow upon it, they stir it not
from its place." Wisdom once appeared in the guise of a
teacher and said: "Knowledge without common sense is
folly; without method it is waste; without kindness it is
fanaticism; without belief in God it is death. But with
common sense, it is wisdom; with method it is power; with
character it is beneficence; with belief in God it is virtue,
life and peace."

Perek differentiates between an uncultured man and a
wise man. "There are seven marks of an uncultured man
and seven of a wise man. The wise man does not speak before
him who is greater than he is in wisdom; and does not
break in upon the speech of his fellow; he is not hasty to
answer; he questions according to the subject matter, and
answers to the point; he speaks upon the first thing first,
and upon the last thing last; regarding that which he has
not understood, he says, 'I do not understand it'; and he

acknowledges the truth. The reverse of all this is to be found in an uncultured man."

Today, people believe that money is the key to happiness. They devote the years of their life to the search for material wealth. But, unfortunately, after acquiring it, they learn that they must still continue their search for happiness. What, then, is the secret of happiness—love, health, fame, power, or wealth?

My son, consult the Book of Proverbs for the answer. The formula might be found in—

"Happy is the man that findeth wisdom,
And the man that obtaineth understanding.
For the merchandise of it is better than the merchandise of
   silver,
And the gain thereof better than fine gold."

This is practical counsel for earthly happiness. If one is wise and righteous, one will be happy. Happiness is not wealth alone. A Hebrew scholar once advised, "There is no wealth like generosity, no treasure like wisdom, no glory like self-mastery, no sin like pride, no poverty like the love of money—no ornament like health." Perhaps Rabbi Bunam summarized this thought with this capsule of wisdom: "Everyone must have two pockets, so that he can reach into the one or the other, according to his needs. In his right pocket are to be the words, "For my sake was the world created," and in his left, "I am but dust and ashes."

My son, select your friends with care. Love the wise and attach yourself to them. Keep away from a wicked neighbor and from those whose reputation is evil. The Japanese have an ingenious way of changing the color and appearance of birds and animals. For example, white sparrows are produced by selecting a pair of grayish birds and keeping them in a white cage, in a white room, where they are attended by a person dressed in white. The psychological effect on a series of generations of birds results in completely white birds. In similar fashion you can make your life strong, pure, holy and sweet in thought, word and action, by an unbroken association with those who live on a higher plane.

The story of the foolish stork also illustrates my point. A farmer's corn was destroyed by the cranes that fed in his field. Annoyed, the farmer set a net to ensnare the birds. When he visited the snare he discovered a beautiful stork caught with the cranes.

"Spare me," pleaded the stork. "I am innocent, indeed I am. I never touched any of your belongings."

"You may be telling the truth," answered the farmer, "but you are in the company of the cranes and I judge you accordingly."

Be careful of the company you keep, for by your friends are you often judged. Choose friends who understand you, know your shortcomings and yet remain your friends.

Remember the teaching of *Ecclesiastes* that a good name is better than precious oil. Our rabbis explained this by saying: Good oil evaporates and becomes less and less, but a good name becomes greater and greater; good oil is used only at times, but a good name is used daily; good oil can be bought for money, but a good name comes unbought to all who deserve it; good oil can be used only by the living, but a good name endures even after death; good oil can be owned only by the rich, but a good name by rich and poor alike, if they truly deserve it.

My son, make your books your companions. Let your bookcases and shelves be your pleasure grounds and gardens. Bask in their paradise, gather their fruit, pluck their roses. Reading is to the mind what exercise is to the body.

It will support you when all other recreations are gone. It will make your hours pleasant to you as long as you live.

"A book is a garden," writes Henry Ward Beecher. "A book is an orchard. A book is a storehouse. It is good company. It is a counselor. It is a multitude of counselors. The best things that the best men have ever thought in past times, and expressed in the best manner, lie in books; and he who knows how to use these may be said, almost, to have control of the world. I would give more for the ownership of books than for that of all the gold in California, if in ownership I sought happiness—various, self-respecting happiness, continuous amidst care and burdens and disappointments in youth, in middle age, and in old age. There is nothing like a book to one who knows how to pluck fruit from it, and how to prepare it for his palate."

My son, have a task to do which will enrich you, and without which the world will feel poorer. Try to do whatever you undertake to do a little better than you have ever done it before. Remember, work without vision is drudgery. A vision without work is only a day-dream. Vision with work is a success story. In whatever you do, you should feel a sense of purpose and a sense of achieving your personal goals.

There is a legend about the man who watched the builders of the Temple at work. He approached one of the masons and asked, "What are you doing?" The mason replied, "Foolish man, can't you see that I am merely cutting stone!" The wise man approached a second worker and repeated the question. "I am working for two *shekalim* a day so that I can feed and clothe my family," was his answer. When the same question was put to a third man, he replied, "What am I doing? Why I am helping to build the Temple of God."

Don't be discouraged by mistakes. Think of a mistake

as only a detour toward your goal. It does not mean that you can't get back to the main road again. The path of progress is pebbled with mistakes that you can turn into stepping stones. Never let the fear of failure prevent you from making decisions. There are many ways of becoming a failure, but never taking a chance is the surest way.

Judge every man charitably and use your best efforts to find a kindly explanation for his conduct. Be tolerant and humble to all. Do not gossip. Speak no scandal, listen to none, for if there were no receivers there would be no bearers of slander.

Visit the sick! When your grandma was ill, I realized the great need for observing this *mitzva*. Visiting the sick makes the invalid feel worthwhile, remembered. It helps lighten pain.

Comfort the mourners! Visit with them. Speak to them. Make their burden a bit easier to bear.

Honor your mother both in word and deed so that blessing may come upon you. Our sages and patriarchs honored their mothers. The world has placed mother on a pedestal. Read a few of the statements made by the great men of the world.

"All that I am or hope to be, I owe to my angel mother" —Abraham Lincoln.

"The world was made darker and sadder when my mother died, but heaven was made brighter and happier"— E. L. Jamison.

"All that is good in my life has come from my mother" —Dwight L. Moody.

My son, as you go through life remember to give service to others. The story is told of a little Chinese girl who was carrying her brother on her back. "Is he heavy?" she was asked. "No," she answered, "he is my brother."

As long as you can help someone, you are of use to the world. There is a lesson to be learned in the story of the great king who made a feast and sent messengers to all the cities and towns in his kingdom, asking the people to come, and promising not only food but wealth.

In one town there was a strong, robust man, who, unfortunately, was blind; and he loudly bemoaned the fact that his affliction would prevent him accepting the king's invitation. But presently he heard that in the same town was a lame man, who was also grieving that he would be unable to go to the feast.

The blind man and the lame man, therefore, came to an arrangement by which the blind man would carry the lame man to the feast, the lame man directing the blind. So the man who had sight but could not walk guided the man who could walk but could not see, and the two went together to the king's feast.

Finally, my son, I want to give you the father's blessings found in *Hayye Adam*: "May God make thee as Ephraim and Manasseh. May it be the will of our Father who is in heaven, to place His love and fear in your heart. May the fear of God be before you all the days of your life, so that you will not sin; and may your delight be in the Torah and in the commandments. May your eyes look straight ahead. May your mouth speak wisdom, and your heart contemplate fear. May your hands be engaged in keeping the commandments, and your legs run to do the will of your Father in heaven. May He give you sons and daughters who are righteous and engaged in the study of the Torah and in keeping the commandments all their days. May your spring be blessed; and may God allow you to find your rightful sustenance in ease and with plenty, beneath His broad hand, and not through the gift of flesh and blood. May your livelihood be one which will set you free for the service of God; and may you be inscribed and sealed for a good life and a long one, in the midst of all the righteous of Israel. Amen."

CHAPTER THIRTY-THREE

A Father Speaks at His Son's Graduation

IN MY many years of high school and parochial school experience, I have participated in perhaps 70 or more commencement exercises. Each one of these thrilled me with the vision and the realization of true accomplishment, of sincere guidance, of genuine character training. It was never too difficult for me to address a group of graduates and to offer my humble advice. Yet tonight, on this rather special occasion, I find myself somewhat at a loss. There surges up within me a torrent of feelings, so strong and so deep, that words to express them come with hesitation and difficulty.

If I have attended other exercises with happiness, you can imagine with what greater joy I attend this one! If I have poured my love and life into the lives of other classes, think to what degree I give my love to this one! If I have glowed with happiness at the accomplishments of previous groups; if I have given God's blessings to other students, how much more so this evening—because this class I truly remember from kindergarten days. It isn't too difficult for me to visualize a morning eight years ago when I saw you all lined up in the sandy school yard, eagerly and fearfully awaiting your first day at school. I remember how I looked at each one of you intently. You, and my own son, were going to go through school together. How I prayed to God that He would spare me so that I could travel the road of education together with you! How many times I visualized

201

and dreamt of tonight's festivities, I cannot even dare to guess. Each year as I attended a Yeshivah graduation, I thought of your class. If I were to make a confession tonight, I would say that in fond fancy I've really issued you diplomas several times; that I've made my commencement speech to this class during the middle hours of many a night. Yet now, though I desperately want to leave you with a meaningful message of understanding, of love, of encouragement and pleasure, I have to grope to find the proper words.

What can I say tonight when I am engulfed with two deep and powerful emotions; when I find myself attending tonight's graduation exercises both as principal and father! What message can I give you? What precepts can I impart? What love can I send out to you? What single thought and hope can I leave with you, whom I've come to love as my very own, who very often have made my home their home, who have not only shared my hours and days here, but my time at home as well.

Earlier this evening one of you said that you would carry the torch of Torah high; that you would pass it from your hands to the hands of your waiting children because you felt that you were not merely graduates of our beloved school, but true students of *Yiddishkeit*. That was a wonderful thought. It must be taken seriously, because in this sad generation some 6,000,000 Jews, who might have passed on God's work, were wiped out. Six million of our people— not a mass like a cup of water composed of six million drops but six million separate individuals, six million human souls.

Count them one by one. Count them as you'd count the flowers of a field, grains of sand, the stars of heaven, the sheep of the flock, the letters of a book. How many days and nights would it take to count six million? Count the six million men, women and children—fathers, mothers, wives, husbands, sons, daughters—count them as individuals with nerves and blood and muscles, with hopes and joys. Count them as they weep, as they shriek, as they tremble, as they die. Count them and then let us make up our minds to take their places in Orthodox Jewry, for we are a deathless people. We must survive. We will survive! Each one of us has a mission in Israel, a sacred mission to carry on the battle for Israel and Torah Judaism.

Let me paraphrase the words of an immortal American, Abraham Lincoln, and say, "Let us here resolve that these honored dead shall not have died in vain." Let us proclaim to the world that they gave their lives on the altar of *Kiddush HaShem*. To each of us here is given this opportunity —an opportunity which is also an example of the unconquerable spirit of Judaism—to dream, to build, to accomplish so that Judaism will be a stronger, brighter force in a braver, newer world for us and for our children.

Jews need not apologize to the nations of the world. No longer do we have to explain why our way of life is advisable. A lesson can be learned from the man who visited the Museum of Art. He looked long at a masterpiece and exclaimed to the attendant, "I don't know why this picture is so famous."

"Sir," replied the attendant, "this picture is no longer being tested. It has lived on through the ages and has been approved by critics of all countries. Millions and millions of men, women, and children have gazed at it in rapture. This picture has withstood all tests and is no longer on trial; but you are."

The Jewish way of life has been tested by the ages. Our way of life has been approved by our fathers—by our scholars of all generations. Rashi, Maimonides, Nachmanides have written and taught the beauty of *Shabbas, kashruth,* our relationships with our fellow man. Our Torah institutions have been a beacon light to the nations of the world. Our Torah has breathed the spark of life into many people. We have lived with the hope that God Almighty will some day see fit to redeem us.

There was once a man who betrothed himself to a beautiful maiden and then went away, and the maiden waited and he came not. Friends and rivals mocked her and said, "He will never come."

She went into her room and took out the letters in which he had promised to be ever faithful. Weeping, she read them and was comforted. In time he returned, and inquiring how she had kept her faith so long, she showed him his letters.

Israel in misery, in captivity, was mocked by the nations for her hopes of redemption; but Israel went into her schools and synagogues and took out the letters, and was comforted. God would in time redeem her and say, "How could you alone, among all the mocking nations, be faithful?"

Then Israel would point to the Law and the Prophets and answer, "Had I not your promise here?"

Graduates, you are going to be the men of the great tomorrow. Whatever you sow, the man of tomorrow shall reap. So, be strong and true. Be generous in praise and appreciation of others; impute worthy motives even to enemies. Give without expectation of return; practice humility, tolerance and self-respect; make the best use of time and opportunity; keep your mind pure and your judgment charitable. Despise not any man. Separate not yourself from the community and judge not your neighbor until you have come into his place. Read, study, and follow the Torah.

A certain wealthy man, who was very miserly, had a

vast fortune of gems and precious stones. Fearing that someone might be tempted to rob him of them, he buried them
in the ground, not far from his home. One day, wanting to
make certain that they were still safe, he sent his servant
to go and dig them up. In the meantime he stood by the
window, waiting. When he saw the servant approaching,
weighted down by the heavy burden, perspiring and grunting, he clasped his hands in despair, and cried, "Alas, my
treasure is gone, and in its place someone has placed ordinary stones."

His son, who was standing at his side, asked, "Father,
how do you know that the servant is not carrying the sack
with the gems inside?"

"No, no my son," said he with a cry of anguish, "were
he carrying precious stones, gems and jewels, he would not
be grunting so, nor would his load appear so burdensome."

Graduates, you have been bedecked with precious gems.
You have been immersed in the study of Torah for the past
eight years. You have been taught the wealth of joy and
real living found in our holy writings. You have dipped into
Chumash, pored over the *Gemorah*, studied Solomon's wisdom, discussed our commentaries. What garments of truth
and beauty you wear! It is the wish of your rabbis and
teachers that you go into the world, into higher spheres of
education, proclaiming that you will uphold the Torah.
God grant you the strength and the time to accomplish this!

CHAPTER THIRTY-FOUR

Defeat Is Not Failure

THIS is not only an age of crisis and destruction, but of deep discouragement as well. As you read your daily newspaper and learn of the brutality that is being practiced, you might well fear that civilization may be doomed. All that is precious in life seems to be threatened by those who are inhuman. So great has this anxiety grown that many people are becoming defeatists. They have come to feel that "what is to be, will be," that they are but small cogs in a machine over which they have little control. Ella Wheeler Wilcox, a popular poet some years ago, counseled:

" 'Tis easy enough to be pleasant
When life flows along like a song.
But the man worthwhile is the man
who will smile
When everything goes dead wrong."

The fact is that there is no work in the world which is just one sweet song. You will never find a job which is agreeable in all its phases and every hour of the day. Whether you are a student or an employee, you will be called upon to do unpleasant tasks, or you will meet with defeat in some particular job. "Our strength grows out of weakness," writes Emerson. "When man is pushed, tormented, defeated, he has a chance to learn something; he has been put on his wits, on his manhood; he has gained facts; learns his ignorance; is cured of the insanity of conceit; has got moderation and real skill." With hard work comes understanding. The obscure pages and problems become clear. The world wants men and women equipped to move forward over the rough roads as well as the smooth.

Many of our greatest leaders have failed repeatedly before finally achieving success. Their ability to meet failure and not let it get them down seemed to strengthen their character. You are all probably familiar with the tale of the Scottish leader, Bruce, who was very discouraged because his men had lost so many battles. As he was trying to rest, he noticed a spider spinning a web. Over and over again the spider spun a thread which broke repeatedly. Finally the spider was successful. Bruce thought if a spider could keep on trying, so could he—and he went out to lead his men— this time in a successful attack.

One of our greatest presidents, Abraham Lincoln, proved he knew how to be defeated without considering it failure. He lost when he first ran for the Legislature in Illinois and also when he attempted to win the nomination for Congress. He was defeated for the United States Senate and was unsuccessful when he ran for Vice President. He failed in business and it took him many years to repay the debts resulting from this failure. He suffered a great personal loss when the young lady whom he had loved and to whom he had been engaged, died.

However, Lincoln never allowed himself to be discouraged. He did not permit his many disappointments and frustrations to get him down. His ability to lose gracefully and his perseverance and determination to win made him one of the greatest leaders America has ever produced. Lincoln believed in the advice offered by Buxton, "The road to success is not to be run upon by seven-leagued boots. Step by step, little by little, bit by bit—that is the way to wealth, that is the way to wisdom, that is the way to glory."

"I think I can," are four magic words that, when woven into the fiber of our human thoughts, can make all the difference as to whether we succeed or fail.

If you are so soft of fiber that you turn aside whenever you reach anything which is difficult you will never get very far. Enjoy your work but do not lie down on the job whenever you come to something which is difficult. Get the habit of mastering your work. Do a good job every hour of the day and every day of the year. The secret of success is not too difficult: do better work than any other man in your field—and keep on doing it. The sturdiest tree is not found in the shelter of a forest, but high upon some rocky crag where its daily battle with the elements shapes it into a thing of beauty.

Discouragement is the road to failure. George Eliot warns, "The only failure a man ought to fear is failure in cleaving to the purpose he sees best." Failures can be divided into several classes—those who thought and never did; those who did and never thought; and those who neither thought nor did.

One of the saddest experiences which can ever come to a man is to awaken, near the end of an unproductive career, to the fact that all through the years he has been using only a small part of himself; that he did not turn his stumbling blocks into stepping stones. Unfortunately he had not learned that life is a stern struggle and a man has to be able to stand up to the buffeting. Allan Hunter tells of a friend who watched a small lemur when a dog came into the room. The little monkey-like creature was so terribly frightened that its long tail became violently agitated. But only for a moment. The tail had to be brought under control. Otherwise the little animal's energy would have been consumed in wagging its unruly tail. Apparently sensing this, the lemur grabbed its tail and held it firmly in its paws until the terrifying experience could be assimilated. We human beings can see the parable. When we are faced with a defeat, we often start wagging our tongues or shaking our knees, or rushing about restlessly, until flustered and frightened, we lose control of ourselves and that only brings on failure. How true is the statement that reads, "Genius takes pains, improves by practice, suffers failures, succeeds often on a second or third try." We owe our rich standard of living to the inventors who were spurred on by their defeats.

He who would experience success must arm himself with four vital and most necessary tools. First, he must have ceaseless industry; second, he must have limitless ambition of purpose; third, he must possess unquenchable enthusiaasm; fourth, he must learn to accept defeat as a step toward eventual success. Given these four, and something else beside—the gift of imagination—it would not matter whether the life of the man began in a shoestore or a grocery store, he would deserve the success that eventually would be his. "Our spirits grow gray before our hairs," observed Charles Lamb. Discouragement comes to old and young alike. Things often go contrary to our dreams and plans. The major cause of failure is discouragement. Restore confidence and take on new heart.

Among the students at a well known college was a young man on crutches. A homely fellow, he had a talent for friendliness and optimism. He won many scholastic honors and the respect of his classmates. One day a classmate asked the cause of his deformity.

When the young invalid said briefly, "Infantile paralysis," the friend questioned further.

"With a misfortune like that, how can you face the world so confidently?"

"Oh," replied the young man on crutches, "the disease never touched my heart."

CHAPTER THIRTY-FIVE

The Gift of Life

UNDER modern conditions of living, people are obliged to work closely together. Their lives intertwine. Everyone is affected deeply by the way other people act and by the things they say. They are all dependent to a large extent upon the acts, habits, attitudes, and policies of others. This is the way our society is constructed, that society which we call civilized. The more well-intentioned, sensitive, and far-seeing individuals adjust themselves to this kind of society. Realizing that the world will prosper only if there is cooperation, they cooperate. They say things which are pleasing rather than irritating. They attempt to give pleasure to others as well as to themselves. They understand that each man is his brother's keeper and so make themselves helpful unto others, thus bringing out their own good points, and putting the *human* into their *being*.

There is real art in enjoying the blessings of life, an art which must be mastered if we are to take advantage of the years allotted to us. However, it is not a difficult art requiring years of collegiate study. At the outset it must be realized that whatever we have is a gift from the Almighty, and that with each oncoming day the gift is renewed.

The wisdom of living consists in making the most of what we have. One person gets nothing but discord out of a piano; another gets harmony. No one claims the piano is at fault. Life is about the same. The discord is there and the harmony is there. If we study life correctly, it will give forth beauty; if we play it false, it will give forth ugliness. Life is not at fault.

We must understand that life is a journey towards an end on this earth, and that this earth is but a vestibule for life to come. We might think of God as the landlord; we are his tenants; life is the lease. He owns the earth and we occupy it. The rent we pay is the service we render to each other. Everything we see, anything we touch, was put on this earth by God; much of it to be fashioned by us for our use in helping others.

Rabbi Abraham J. Feldman had this thought in mind when he prepared a pamphlet for the personnel of the Jewish faith in the Armed Forces of the United States.

"The earth is the Lord's, and the fullness thereof; the world, and they that dwell therein" (Psalms 24:1). "The earth hath He given to the children of men" (Psalms 115:16). Rabbi Feldman then goes on to describe life as a sort of world-estate with the Almighty being the proprietor. It is a spacious estate and has room enough for all people. It has everything needed for an abundant rich life.

We are reminded that the earth is the Lord's. Everyone is welcome on this estate, which He has given us for our benefit, placing very few restrictions on its use.

There are millions and millions of people on this estate, all with varied capacities and gifts, and all welcome guests of the gracious host. For our guidance, to avoid conflicts, for the assurance of individual and collective happiness, for the sake of orderliness, to promote human dignity, a set of rules has been posted by the owner, whereby we, as tenants, may govern our lives and conduct on this world-estate.

The rules of life are really exceedingly simple, and are known to civilization as the Ten Commandments. Rabbi

Rosenfeld restates them in modern terms, and in the form of a lease.

RULE I

Remember:

There is an owner on this estate and you are not He: "I am the Lord." "The earth is the Lord's . . . the world, and they that dwell therein."

RULE II

Remember:

You are not to forget that even though you do not see Him, He watches over you at all times. Any misstep that you make to ignore His ownership may affect you and your children, to the third and fourth generations after you.

RULE III

Remember:

You should be respectful towards your host, respectful and courteous. This is only ordinary decency.

RULE IV

Remember:

While you are expected to labor and help develop this estate you are not to be in perpetual motion. To be sure, you must work; but you must also learn to enjoy this world. "The earth hath He given to the children of men." You must not only dig and explore and produce; you must take time to look around, to think. You cannot do this very well if you are constantly at work and endlessly in motion. Hence, pause at regular intervals, once in seven days. Get your bearings. Communicate leisurely with the owner. He expects it. Catch your breath on the Sabbath. Be a free man! Do not permit yourself to become like an animal, forever on a treadmill. Observe the Sabbath rest.

RULE V
Remember:

In the course of many generations, the owner of the world-estate has found that His most trusted agents and representatives are those who are parents. They are links between the generations. They are the custodians of the wisdom and experience of the past. And so the Fifth Rule bids us show a deep regard—honor—for our parents, through whom He works. It is suggested to us that we ought to do it so "that your days may be prolonged on the land which the Lord your God gives you."

RULE VI
Remember:

Every life is as precious as yours, and every man has as much right to his life as you have to yours. Be very careful, therefore, that no one loses his life because of you.

RULE VII
Remember:

Your home on this estate must be kept pure and sacred. But remember also that your neighbor's home is as sacred as yours. Do not pollute or desecrate any man's home. Adultery, like adulteration, cheapens, changes, dilutes, and weakens life.

Rule VIII
Remember:

The right to possess the necessities of life and the fruits of one's labor on this estate were granted to all of us alike. You have the right to own, possess. But all other men have an identical right. Be very careful that no one deprive another of the right of such possession or take another's rightful possession from him.

Rule IX
Remember:

You are all interdependent. The security of one man is the security of all. Have regard, therefore, for each other. Respect your neighbor! Be careful lest any word or act of yours misrepresent or malign your neighbor. An evil or unkind word kills the good repute of your fellow-tenant. It instills hate and causes prejudice or bigotry to flame where love and justice alone should prevail.

Rule X
Remember:

If you want happiness on this estate take care not to be greedy. Emulate your neighbor if you can. Be ambitious! Achieve as he has achieved, if you can. But be not covetous and do not attempt to gain anything for yourself at the cost of depriving others of what is rightfully theirs.

The above are ten rules of life restated by Rabbi Feldman. They are basic rules governing our stay on earth. They are simple, sensible rules not at all difficult to live by. They create the possibility of an abundant, happy, peaceful life for all. They call for an understanding of our neighbor's rights. They imply the happiness that might be ours if we learn to live with and appreciate our fellow-tenants.

Once a man went to call at the place of business of one of his friends, a jeweler with a large clientele. The jeweler showed his friend a store of superb diamonds among other precious stones. Among them was a stone so lusterless that the friend said: "That one has no beauty at all."

"Hasn't it?" asked the jeweler, lifting the stone from the tray and closing his fist over it. In a few minutes, when he opened his hand, the stone glowed with all the splendor of the rainbow.

"Why, what have you done to it?" asked the friend.

The jeweler smiled. "That is an opal," he said. "It is what we call a sympathetic jewel. It needs only to be gripped with the human hand to bring out all its wonderful beauty."

One of the finest aspects of living is liking people and wanting to share activities in the human enterprise. The greatest pleasures come through giving pleasure to those who work with us, to the person who lives next door, and to those who live under the same roof. A tiny seed, if planted and tended, can produce a pretty flower, a mighty tree, or food in abundance. When we help some *one*, we are helping *two*, for we can feel the joy ourselves.

Life is a great adventure in human relationships. We must learn to acknowledge and appreciate the things that are worthwhile in others. We must learn to cooperate, to share, to understand that our lives are intertwined. Man does not live in a world of his own; his brothers are here also. Unfortunately, there is a great deal of truth in the observation made by the farmer, who after returning from his first visit to the city remarked, "The closer people live together, the farther friends are apart."

If we are to live, we must serve each other. Only through service can man find himself. Only through cooperation can he survive. It is interesting to realize that if we make one person happy every day, in forty years we would have made 14,600 human beings happy for a little time at least.

We live by habit. Have you ever walked through a meadow and found your clothes covered with prickly little seed-heads of burdock? If so, you will have discovered that you cannot shake them off or brush them away. You have to pick them off one by one. That's how it is with habits. They fasten on to the mind, hardening into characteristics, and, like burrs, they cling tenaciously once they have a hold upon you. You cannot easily flick them off. Each one has to be dealt with separately. There are good habits and bad habits, but unfortunately the good ones tend to fall away. It's the bad ones that cling.

Harry Emerson Fosdick wrote: "We ask the leaf, 'Are you complete in yourself?' And the leaf answers, 'No, my life is in the branches.' We ask the branch, and the branch answers, 'No, my life is in the root.' We ask the root, and it answers, 'No my life is in the trunk and the branches and leaves. Keep the branches stripped of leaves, and I shall die.' "

So it is with life. Man must recognize that there are people all around who make living possible. For life at its best, a person must see himself as having a share in something important. In his work, he needs to feel that he is doing something that matters, that he is adding to the lives of the people about him, and that they are helping him survive. Unfortunately, too many people follow the path of least assistance. They keep thinking of the practical Madison Avenue philosophy, "What is in it for me?"

A certain gentleman was being conducted on a tour of

the other world. On reaching the nether regions he was greatly surprised to find the people all seated at a banquet table loaded with appetizing food. On the wall was a sign listing the one law of the place—which was strictly enforced. Everyone must use the knives and forks provided by the management. But the tools of service had such long handles that no one could get a morsel of food near his mouth. They were all starving to death. And that was Hell!

In the celestial city our visiting friend also found the people seated at banquet tables loaded with the same food and holding the same long-handled forks. But they were having a delightful time. They were feeding each other. This was Heaven.

Emily Dickinson capsuled this philosophy in a meaningful four line poem:

> "Who has not found the heaven below
> Will fail of it above.
> God's residence is next to mine,
> His furniture is love."

This is a sad troubled world. No person can question that. To some people it must be a terrifying world, in which the roads to happiness appear to be barred. The future seems vague and unhappy. There doesn't seem to be a bright spot on the horizon. However, one may find some peace of mind even in times of danger, confusion, and turmoil. One rule a person must keep uppermost in his mind is that *conduct* and *conscience* should be tuned in on the same human channel.

The essential teaching of *Sefer B'reshit is menshlichkeit*, the fulfilling of one's duty toward man. Great indeed were the Patriarchs in their devotion to God, in their love of Him, in their fear of Him, in their anticipatory observance of His Torah. But equally great was their love of man, their respect for a human being regardless of race, color, or creed. It was they who first practiced this well-known political doctrine, and it is these practices that have spoken to us most eloquently down the ages—and to the nations of the world, if they but listened. If the nations of the world only practiced *menshlichkeit* the need for the United Nations would be minimized, and heaven would be nearer to earth.

There is an old legend concerning the place where the Temple was built. It relates that two brothers lived on adjoining farms; one was married and the other a bachelor. Their farms were of equal size, and the harvest of one farm was seen to be just as fruitful as the other.

The wheat had been cut and was standing in sheaves in the fields. The married brother, sitting in his home thinking of his bachelor brother, said: "He is a lonely man. He has no wife, no children, no joy in life except in what he buys and sells. I think I will take some of my sheaves and put them over in his field tonight."

It so happened that at the same time the bachelor was thinking of the married brother with his wife and children, and he said: "My brother has many mouths to feed, and I don't need all I have. I'll take some of my sheaves and put them in his field tonight."

Secretly carrying out their plans they met face to face one dark night. The legend says that at the spot where they met the Temple was built, for there heaven was nearest earth.

If we are to live, we must show our love for other people; show it to them in our everyday dealings. We must show consideration and understanding. Unfortunately, when we count an unselfish deed, we count it in worldly terms—in money, effort, what people will think or say.

But who can estimate the good that results from doing some good deed? And who can estimate the loss of a denied urge to help someone? A king placed a heavy stone in the middle of a road. People thronged by, stepped over the boulder, kicked it angrily, murmured, grumbled, but none removed the stone. Finally one man came along, saw the obstacle, picked it up to make the way easier for those who would come after him. Under the stone the king had placed a purse filled with gold.

It may be that we close the door to adventure, laughter, happiness, richness in living, because of the price tags we place on our actions. Perhaps it was this practical philosophy of life that motivated a man to write his own epitaph —"BORN A HUMAN BEING, DIED A WHOLESALE GROCER." When he was asked to explain what he had written, he said: "I was so busy selling groceries that I did not have time to get married, raise a family, and enjoy the company of friends. There was a whole area of life crowded out by the grocery business. I was so busy selling groceries that I didn't have time to travel, even though I had the money. I was so busy selling groceries I did not have time for the theatre, for lectures, for concerts, for classes, for reading, for sermons. I was so busy selling groceries I did not have time for community service—religious, social, or political. All of these areas of life were crowded out by the grocery business. I was so successful, I became a wholesaler. But I was so busy making a living, I never had time to live."

Edward Markham, the inspired philosophical poet, wrote:

> "We are all blind until we see
> That in the human plan
> Nothing is worth the making
> If it doesn't make the man.

Why build these cities glorious,
If man unaided goes?
In vain we build the world, unless
The builder also grows."

CHAPTER THIRTY-SIX

Souls That Live On

*"In memory of Max and Rebecca Schiff and
Jacob and Rosalie Klaus, the parents of my
dear friends Sam and Bessie Klaus."*

D EEP in the heart of every man and woman lies the desire
to achieve immortality ... to perpetuate a name ... to
commit a deed that will multiply itself over and over again
and thus live on. This is mankind's longing for immortality.

There is only one way to get ready for immortality, and
that is to love this life and live it as bravely and faithfully
as we can. There are men and women who live in accordance
with this philosophy. They believe in boys and girls, in the
people of a great and better tomorrow. They believe in the
curse of ignorance, in the dignity of teaching and in the
joy of serving others; in wisdom as revealed in human lives
as well as in the pages of a printed volume. They believe in
lessons taught by example and not merely by precept; in the
ability to work with the hands as well as to think with the
head; in the beauty of the home, in daily life, in laughing,
in ideals and hopes. They believe that every hour of the day
offers a reward and a challenge and that man is God's stake
in human history. They are the dawn and the dusk, the
challenge and the test.

They see life in the light of God and understand that this
world is not centered in puny interests. They understand the
worth of their fellow-men. They accept the challenge of life
to prove that they believe that each human being is a letter

spelling out the name of God. They are ready to sacrifice their own lives so that others might live.

This is the story of sacrifice.

Here men died so that others might live.

It was an early icy February dawn in 1943. The American troopship Dorchester plowed through the churning cold black waters off Greenland. The decks were crowded with American G. I.'s, some of whom were aboard ship for the first time in their lives. There were fathers separated from their wives and families. Who knows what they were thinking about that morning? There were sons, fresh out of college, with some faint trace of their boyish smiles, discussing perhaps the major baseball teams. All together they were young American lads, Jews, Catholics, Protestants, Baptists, though for that moment they all just felt like buddies, like Americans going about their business to make this world a decent place to live in.

Suddenly came the Nazi torpedo, the torpedo that ripped into the heart of the troopship; that cut short all conversations, all thoughts, all smiles. There were screams of the dying, cries of the frightened, and orders from those whose business it was to rescue as many lives as possible. And on the deck in various parts of the ship were four men of God, four men plucked from their parishes by the Hand of God and set together in that icy fog that February. And all at once the fog melted away, and all about them there was light!

First there was Chaplain George Fox. He was the eldest. Up in Vermont they called him Pastor Fox, "The Little Minister." He was only five feet seven inches tall. Back in 1917, he had lied about his age so that he could get into the Marines as a medical corps assistant. At that time he had won a Silver Star for rescuing a wounded soldier from a

battlefield filled with poison gas although he himself had
no gas-mask. Before Chaplain George Fox boarded the Dorchester, he wrote a letter to his little daughter. She received
it after the news that the ship was torpedoed.

"I want you to know," he wrote, "how proud I am that
your marks in school are high, but remember that kindness
and charity and courtesy are much more important."

Then there was Alexander Goode. He had been too young
to be in World War I. At that time he was in Eastern High
School, Washington, D. C. His great desire at that time was
to follow his father's foot-steps and become a rabbi. He
wanted to spread the word of Torah, the idea of love, brotherhood, and concern for others. While training for the rab-
binate, Alex Goode joined the National Guard. He married
his childhood sweetheart, and they had four children. He
loved his family and home. He loved his congregation. He
loved his work. He often quoted from the Talmud, "I am
the creature of God, and so is my fellow-man; my calling
is in the town, and his in the fields; I go early to my work,
and he to his; he does not boast of his labor nor I of mine,
and if thou wouldst say, 'I accomplish great things and he
little things,' we have learned that whether a man accom-
plishes great things or small, his reward is the same if only
his heart be set upon Heaven." After Rabbi Goode got his
pulpit, he felt he was not too worthy. He felt he would know
better how to heal men's souls if he knew how to heal their
bodies too; and so for three years, he drove every day to
Johns Hopkins University, forty-five miles away, until he
won his medical degree.

Johnny Washington, the little Irish boy from Newark,
New Jersey was also on the Dorchester. Johnny loved
music and sang in the church choir. Johnny was always
laughing, right through his training as a priest. Even after

he was ordained, he played handball in the street with the boys from his parish. He organized basketball teams. When the war came along, and his boys went into the Army, Father Johnny went right along with them as a matter of course. They say that when the Dorchester went down, he was still laughing . . . laughing and singing and praying to comfort those who could not reach the lifeboats. He was making the greatest sacrifice man is called upon to make. He was dying so that others might live.

Clark Poling was the youngest of our four men of God. Dr. Daniel A. Poling, his father, remembers that Clark was a boy who always loved peace and brotherhood. He was the eighth in an unbroken line of ministers of the Gospel. He was ordained a minister in the Dutch Reformed Church and was assigned to a pulpit in Schenectady. He married and later in life was delighted by the birth of two sons who would carry on the heritage of ministers of God. When the war came along young Clark became a Chaplain. His last letter to his wife had a note of complaint. He feared that though the Dorchester would carry him to a training camp in England, he would never have a chance to slough through the mud and blood and misery of war itself. He wanted to be near the men when they needed him.

And so these four men—Protestant, Catholic, and Jew—from four different towns; the country boy from Vermont, the city boy from Washington, the slum kid from Newark, and the parson's son from New York City, met on the slanting deck of the Dorchester. It was a rendezvous with death but a rendezvous with God too; and their voices rose above the cold green swirling waters.

"Our father, who are in heaven, hallowed be Thy name."
"Shema Yisroel Adoshem Elokenu, Adoshem Echod."

"Hear, O Israel, The Lord our God, The Lord is one."
"Have mercy on me, O God, according to Thy great
mercy, Thy kingdom come . . . Thy will be done."

These four men walking the decks of the Dorchester that
morning heard the blast and knew what would happen. They
walked the decks giving help and comfort. They didn't question the men, asking them what religion they professed.
They knew that all were children of God and that all needed
help. They felt that they had been put there that morning to
show the world that all faiths were one; that all faiths were
meant to instill the love of God in human beings.

Let the words of the poet Joseph Auslander, tell the rest
of the story as he did in the Saturday Evening Post . . .

"That morning, in the cold grey light
Off Greenland where the icebergs churned,
Their ship was blasted; stiff and white,
The troops stood frozen stark with fright;
The fearsome waters boiled and burned.

Swiftly the four priests comforted
The frantic, urged them to the floats,
Quieted terror, blessed the dead,
Prayed, strapped the boys in lifebelts, led
The wounded, helped them to the boats.

They asked of no man whence he came,
Or at what altar did he pray;
Gentile and Jew were all the same
Before their eyes; they spoke God's name
And gave their own life belts away.

Four men of God went down at sea
Washington, Poling, Fox, and Goode,
Bound by a passion for liberty
And a burning faith that keeps men free
In the bond of human brotherhood."

CHAPTER THIRTY-SEVEN

Heaven on Earth: A Tribute to Bertha Zelinger

WE always speak and write of a life made worthwhile, a life devoted to good deeds, to bettering humanity, to making this world a more decent place for our children. We speak about dedication and devotion, about altruistic motives, about building institutions of God and man, about improving the universe by our presence, and leaving it a better place than we found it.

We speak and write about *Bertha Zelinger*. Her life is a story wrought in deeds. It is a story of human endeavor—of actions, dreams and visions. She built her home so that the values of the Patriarchs would prevail. Her life was lived in accordance with the ideals of our forefathers, of Abraham, Isaac and Jacob. She did not care only for herself but was concerned about the happiness and welfare of her neighbors. She blended her life with that of the community. She combined her past memories with her future hopes and aspirations. It was her tremendous faith which helped Toras Emes, and which launched the Kaminetzer Mesifta. She saw the beauty of life, but always with a clear vision of what was beyond the horizon. She built a life out of God, Torah, people, and fused it with her unending zeal.

Her life illustrated—if we did not know it before—that God is not found in "far off realms of space" or "heights of upper air," but in the soul of a human being.

God said, "Let there be light," and light there was in

the home Bertha made . . . light that gave warmth and spiritual guidance . . . light that gave inspiration and wisdom . . . light that gave truth, peace and love . . . light that was shed by one of God's angels on earth.

There is only one kind of beauty that can transcend time, and Bertha Zelinger possessed it. It is, of course, beauty of the spirit that lights the eyes and transforms a woman into a single letter of God's law. Bertha Zelinger had one desire and that was to lose herself in the lives of her dear ones, and in the problems of all who came to her door. Nothing was beneath her. She would solicit for a bazaar, clothing for the unfortunate, collect money to set someone up in business, arrange a match between a widow and a widower, make peace between friends, run meetings, attend charitable affairs, organize auxiliaries, call and infuse others with the love of Torah—all this, and yet be a devoted mother and a loving, dedicated wife.

There is a story told about the first time a locomotive engine pulled into a small town. The Hasidim decided to show this tremendous advance in scientific and mechanical genius to their Rebbe. As the Rebbe neared the station to inspect this modern means of transportation, he saw a long line of black, cold, somber-looking cars attached to each other. The engine in front was belching fire. The boiler was hot; smoke was rising from its short chimney. Suddenly, with a tremendous roar, black clouds of smoke rose heavenward, the engine started moving, and the long line of trains moved along with it.

"Rebbe, Rebbe, what do you say to this wonderful sight?"

The Rebbe appeared to be lost in thought for a moment and then replied softly, "Look how one hot, fiery creation can pull along so many cold ones!"

Isn't this the same with human beings? One person, consumed with zeal and love for Torah, can ignite the souls of many about her. Bertha Zelinger was full of spiritual fire and Torah enthusiasm, and brightened the *Ner Tamid* in Jewish souls.

Bertha believed in God.
Bertha believed in the word of God.
She believed in the family altar.
She believed in the holiness of man.
She believed in the sanctity of motherhood.
She believed in the concern for the spiritual welfare of others.

She believed in building schools which would teach the Word of God.

Bertha had something of God in the immensity of her love, and much of an angel in her tireless solicitude for the welfare of others. Years ago, she discovered the secret of life. It was caring for the happiness of others. It was concern for her fellow-man. It was sharing God's gift with others. It was planting trees, the fruit of which future generations would enjoy. It was looking out of the window and seeing people, instead of looking into the mirror and seeing only oneself.

Bertha was a rare soul. Her entire existence was bound up with the growth of Torah. She planned new buildings, and motivated all her friends to be concerned with Torah institutions. She wanted to share with others her deep abiding love for Orthodoxy. She wanted others to join her in the work of perpetuating a generation of more active, orthodox Jews. She didn't care for diamonds and gems. Her jewels were the many children she helped to a Torah education.

But now, Bertha's heart beats no more. Her precious

soul has been taken from us and we grieve for someone lost. Now we can only remember how empty our lives are and recall how full and rich we were before. We look back on all the many days and years of happiness we enjoyed and we praise God for the treasure He gave us. Today, we cry and bemoan our tremendous loss.

Bertha's heart beats no more and her kindly eyes are closed forever. Thousands mourn as Heaven rejoices. We have lost a friend. Heaven has gained a pure soul. We have a void in our lives; the angels have gained a follower. Bertha is not with us but her spirit lives on. Her nobility, her high hopes, her sincere prayers live on. Her strength, loyalty, and love live on. What she has seeded will be harvested by our children. The cycle she began will be continued.

There is a story told about a person standing at the shore watching a ship depart. Perhaps it can give us some comfort.

I am standing upon the seashore. A ship at my side spreads her white sails to the morning breeze and starts for the blue ocean. She is an object of beauty and strength, and I stand and watch her until at length she is only a ribbon of white cloud just where the sea and the sky come to mingle with each other. Then someone at my side says, "There! She's gone!"

Gone where? Gone from my sight—that is all. She is just as large in mast and hull and spar as she was when she left my side, and just as able to bear her load of living freight—to the place of destination. Her diminished size is in me, not in her, and just at the moment when someone at my side says, "There! She's gone!" there are other voices ready to take up the glad shout, "There! She comes!" And that is Dying.

May all the Torah institutions she built flourish. May all

the children she helped to an education become *talmidim chachomim.* May the light she created never be extinguished. Her wealth can never be dissipated because it is in the lives of the thousands of Yeshivah boys she aided.

May the *heaven on earth* she built be an inspiration to all of us.

CHAPTER THIRTY-EIGHT

Take Hold of the Carrot

A MAN had a striking dream. He dreamed he had ascended the ladder from earth to Heaven. Expectantly he knocked upon the door. Someone responded and demanded, "Who is there?"

Proudly, the man called his name.

"Who is with you?" came the reply.

"No one," answered the man. "I am alone."

"Sorry," said the angel, "but we are instructed never to open these gates for a single individual. Bring another soul with you and both will gain entrance here."

HEAVEN, MAN AND A CARROT, what an odd name for a book! Yet the name, symbolically explained in Chapter I, carries a message. It teaches that the sharing of life's good is the key which opens the gates of Heaven, and which makes this journey through life a pleasant and rewarding experience. It counsels that one should never pass up an opportunity to help others. If we will help our neighbors become better human beings, help them to grow spiritually, emotionally, intellectually, and economically, we cannot avoid helping ourselves in these same ways. Helping others makes for a *heaven on earth*.

According to an old legend, a woman went to Heaven and looked about the streets for her mansion. She saw many beautiful homes, but hers was not among them. At last, on a small side street she saw a tiny cottage. She was told it belonged to her. She was indignant, but an angel said,

"When you were on earth you built a beautiful split-level home, but you sent very little material here for your heavenly home. We only build up here with the material you send up ahead of time."

Life is not made for the accumulation of material wealth alone. The man who lives for himself fails himself and humanity. It is true that he may gain much wealth, position and even power, but he is still a failure. The man who lives for others, who wishes to share God's gifts, has achieved true success. A rich man who consecrates his wealth and his position to the good of humanity is a success. A poor man who gives of his service to others has achieved true success even though material prosperity is never his.

Man must have an altruistic attitude toward life. This type of attitude is like a cork—it buoys you up. A selfish attitude is like lead—it sinks you.

There is a strange plant in South America which finds a moist place and rests there for a while, sending its roots down and becoming green. When this bit of earth dries up, the plant draws itself together and is blown along by the wind until it finds another moist spot, where it repeats the same story. On and on it rolls, stopping wherever it finds a little water and staying until the water is exhausted. But after all its journeyings, it is nothing but a bundle of dead roots and leaves. The life of this plant tells the story of those who drink only at this world's springs. They go on from spring to spring, but at the end of the longest life, they are nothing but bundles of unsatisfied desires and burning thirsts.

Be unselfish and you will be happy. The time to be unselfish is now, the place is here. You needn't be told the way to be unselfish, for the road is clearly marked. Let us all share the meaning of this prayer:

DEAR GOD,

Inject into my life a dash of HUMAN KINDNESS.

And please add some of the BREATH OF VISION that will make me realize that, in truth, I AM MY BROTHER'S KEEPER.

Pour into my soul the OIL OF GRACIOUSNESS—the mark of a compassionate human being.

Give me the INITIATIVE to play well my part in this big, busy world and to so regulate my life that when I pass on no man can say of me: "He lived for self alone."

Bequeath to me a generous amount of GOOD CHEER, so that when my friend and neighbor is weighed down with despair I may go to help him look up and hope anew.

Renew my blood with a transfusion of FAITH so that I can open every heavy heart that comes my way.

Please God, make all the children in this big beautiful world of Yours happy, but don't forget those of us who are in middle age and in the golden years of our lives.

Write upon our hearts a reminder of the carefreeness of youth, of our own tasks in life. Teach us that real happiness consists not of material things, but in days spent in *THE SERVICE OF ONE'S FELLOWS*.

By all means, take hold, hang on to my carrot, and together we will be lifted into God's celestial region, HEAVEN.